A DYNAMIC CASCADE MODEL OF THE DEVELOPMENT OF SUBSTANCE-USE ONSET

Kenneth A. Dodge, Patrick S. Malone, Jennifer E. Lansford,
Shari Miller, Gregory S. Pettit, and John E. Bates

WITH COMMENTARY BY
John E. Schulenberg and
Julie Maslowsky

T0337954

W. Andrew Collins
Series Editor

MONOGRAPHS OF THE SOCIETY FOR RESEARCH IN CHILD DEVELOPMENT

Serial No. 294, Vol. 74, No. 3, 2009

 WILEY-
BLACKWELL   *Boston, Massachusetts*   *Oxford, United Kingdom*

A DYNAMIC CASCADE MODEL OF THE DEVELOPMENT OF SUBSTANCE-USE ONSET

CONTENTS

COMMENTARY

ABSTRACT

Although the onset of illicit substance use during adolescence can hit parents abruptly like a raging flood, its origins likely start as a trickle in early childhood. Understanding antecedent factors and how they grow into a stream that leads to adolescent drug use is important for theories of social development as well as policy formulations to prevent onset. Based on a review of the extant literature, we posited a dynamic cascade model of the development of adolescent substance-use onset, specifying that (1) temporally distinct domains of biological factors, social ecology, early parenting, early conduct problems, early peer relations, adolescent parenting, and adolescent peer relations would predict early substance-use onset; (2) each domain would predict the temporally next domain; (3) each domain would mediate the impact of the immediately preceding domain on substance use; and (4) each domain would increment the previous domain in predicting substance use. The model was tested with a longitudinal sample of 585 boys and girls from the Child Development Project, who were followed from prekindergarten through Grade 12. Multiple variables in each of the seven predictor domains were assessed annually through direct observations, testing, peer nominations, school records, and parent-, teacher-, and self-report. Partial least-squares analyses tested hypotheses. Of the sample, 5.2% had engaged in substance use by Grade 7, and 51.3% of the sample had engaged in substance use by Grade 12. Five major empirical findings emerged: (1) Most variables significantly predicted early substance-use onset; (2) predictor variables were significantly related to each other in a web of correlations; (3) variables in each domain were significantly predicted by variables in the temporally prior domain; (4) each domain's variables significantly mediated the impact of the variables in the temporally prior domain on substance-use outcomes; and (5) variables in each domain significantly incremented variables in the previous domain in predicting substance-use onset. A dynamic cascade represented the most parsimonious model of how substance use develops. The findings are consistent with six features of social development theories: (1) multiple modest effects; (2) primacy of early influences; (3) continuity in adaptation; (4) reciprocal transactional development; (5) nonlinear growth in problem behaviors during sensitive periods; and (6) opportunities for change with each new domain. The findings suggest points for interventions, public policies, and economics of substance-use and future inquiry.

I. INTRODUCTION

In spite of massive efforts, the American war on drugs has not yet been won (Caulkins, Reuter, Iguchi, & Chiesa, 2005; Miron, 2008). Federal, state, and local law enforcement agencies spend over US$44 billion per year in interdiction, prosecution, and incarceration. It is expected that arrests for drug law violations in 2009 will exceed the 1,841,182 arrests of 2007 (Uniform Crime Reports, 2009). Treatment expenditures are also massive. Substance use disorder treatment expenditures exceed US$18 billion per year (Substance Abuse and Mental Health Services Administration, 2005). In spite of these efforts, the rate of substance use disorders has not changed appreciably in the past decade. Data from 2004 to 2007 indicate that 9.7% of adults aged 18 and older in the United States need treatment for a substance use problem as defined by the Diagnostic and Statistical Manual of Mental Disorders (Substance Abuse and Mental Health Services Administration, July 2, 2009). The rate among young adults aged 18–25 is over double that rate, at 21.1% of the population (Substance Abuse and Mental Health Services Administration, June 25, 2009).

During adolescence, problem behaviors, especially alcohol, tobacco, and other drug (ATOD) use, coalesce (Johnston, O'Malley, Bachman, & Schulenberg, 2008) and become costly in treatment, lost wages, and crime (Miller, 2004). Underage drinking alone costs the United States US$53 billion annually (National Research Council, 2004). The U.S. Office of National Drug Control Policy (1999) indicates that substance-use-related economic costs total US$377 billion annually and are on the rise. Miller (2004) estimated the annual cost of multiproblem youth at over US$400 billion. Cohen (2005) estimated the lifetime cost per adolescent persistent drug abuser at US$970,000, and the social–psychological consequences are even more devastating (Kendall & Kessler, 2002; Kessler et al., 2001).

These enormous costs, and the failure of law enforcement and treatment programs, have led to modest prevention efforts. Cohen (2005) has cited simulation experiments that show that American taxpayers would endorse higher levels of funding for prevention if, and only if, programs were

1

first proven effective. Unfortunately, prevention programs have not yet demonstrated large-scale success (Ennett et al., 2003). School-based prevention efforts have received most of their funding from the Safe and Drug-Free Schools and Communities Act (Modzeleski, 2006). When the predecessor to this legislation was first enacted in 1986, it provided US$490 million for the DARE program. The program reached its zenith in 1992, when it received $502 million and penetrated virtually every public school system in the country. Randomized-controlled trials later proved DARE to be ineffective (Ennett et al., 1994). Although other programs have since proven efficacious in small experiments, at-scale prevention efforts have not yet realized effective impact (Ennett et al., 2003).

Toward the goal of developing empirically based prevention programs, epidemiologic studies have proliferated. These studies have taken largely a risk-factor approach following from the pioneering methods of Rutter and Garmezy (1983), in which individual-difference variables in childhood are statistically linked to later substance use. Empirical research has identified several dozen factors in childhood that enhance risk for substance use during adolescence (reviewed by Dahl & Spear, 2004; Hawkins, Catalano, & Miller, 1992; National Research Council, 2004; Weinberg, Rahdert, Colliver, & Glantz, 1998; Zucker, 2006b), but a laundry list of risk factors has not yet led to efficacious prevention programs. Although numerous theories of substance-use onset that compile these factors have been offered (e.g., Brook, Brook, Gordon, Whiteman, & Cohen, 1990; Catalano, Kosterman, Hawkins, Newcomb, & Abbott, 1996; Simons, Conger, & Whitbeck, 1988), none has sufficiently explained the developmental–transactional relations among risk factors and the ecological transitions that a child goes through on a path toward substance use in order to guide strategic preventive intervention (see Petraitis, Flay, & Miller, 1995, for a review of theories). The goals of this monograph are to (1) articulate a developmental theory that integrates the extant literature; (2) subject the proposed model to rigorous empirical testing through prospective inquiry; and (3) provide implications of the findings for prevention practice and public policy.

CONTEMPORARY THEORIES OF ADOLESCENT DEVELOPMENT

Moving well beyond the cataloguing of risk factors and the contentious debate between nature and nurture, contemporary theories build on Sameroff and Chandler's (1975) seminal transactional model and updated treatise (Sameroff, 2009) to emphasize the dynamic relations between the individual and multiple social contexts across development from birth through adolescence. Lerner and Castellino (2002) have noted, "(T)he forefront of contemporary developmental theory and research is associated with theoretical ideas stressing that the systemic dynamics of individual-context relations provide the bases of behavior and developmental change" (p. 124).

Theorists of development have articulated concepts of reciprocal influences, mediational mechanisms, transactional exchanges, dynamical systems, and interaction effects that cumulate over time. Gottlieb (1997) introduced the term coaction to describe the coordinated exchanges between a child and the environment across development. Dahl and Spear (2004) have described how rapid brain development during adolescence leads the youth to be especially influenced by environmental stimuli that alter brain structure, which, in turn, leads the youth to turn toward specific appealing environments. Steinberg et al. (2006) have provided a map for how myriad genetic, biological, social, and ecological factors conspire to produce disorders in adolescence, including substance abuse. Collectively, these theories tell a story of development that begins with an infant born into a social ecology that both shapes and is shaped by the infant. Brain structures guide the child to gravitate toward compatible and reinforcing environments, but those environments act on the child as well to shape brain development, much like the wind shapes the growth of a tree limb.

The developmental transaction between the child and the environment in emergent behaviors is played out at multiple levels. Microexchanges between a child and parent that occur across minutes tell the story of the onset of aggressive coercive acts (Granic & Patterson, 2006). Daily exchanges between a rapidly growing infant and a physical environment tell the story of the onset of walking (Thelan, Ulrich, & Wolff, 1991), and ongoing social exchanges involving aggression and social rejection that are played out across years tell the story of social–cognitive development (Fontaine, Yang, Dodge, Bates, & Pettit, 2008).

EMPIRICAL TESTING OF THEORIES OF ADOLESCENT DEVIANCE

Although developmental theory has become rich, empirically testing the complex dynamic interplay postulated by Sameroff and Chandler (1975) in the domain of complex phenomena such as adolescent deviance has proven daunting. Most efforts have been restricted to transactions between the child and only one other social unit. For example, Stice and Barrera (1995) found support for a transactional relation between adolescent problem behaviors and parenting, such that lack of parental support and control predicted adolescent substance use, which, in turn, predicted decreases in parental support and control. Dishion and Owen (2002) found

3

support for a transactional model of adolescent substance use and peer processes, in which deviant friendships predicted substance use, which, in turn, predicted later gravitation toward a growing deviant peer culture.

The most well-articulated dynamics systems model of deviant behavioral development has been offered by Granic and Patterson (2006), who described coercive exchanges between a child and a parent that accelerate and mutate into highly aggressive outcomes. Their description is compelling but is restricted to microlevel exchanges of aggression and does not offer a long-term or cross-context model of development from childhood into adolescence. Boker and Graham (1998) used dynamical systems theory to find support for an uncoupled linear oscillator model of frequency of cigarette and alcohol use across time in adolescents. Although they found the theory compelling, they acknowledged that future studies would need to integrate individual difference and environmental factors into a fuller developmental understanding. Gottfredson, Kearley, and Bushway (2008) have effectively integrated transactional models with dynamical systems theory to show that drug use, drug treatment, and crime influence each other across an 11-month period.

Charting transactional relations in microexchanges is important, but theories of development often posit transactional relations at a broader relationship level across longer periods of time. Very few studies have integrated dynamic relations across multiple social systems over long periods of time, and yet this integration is necessary for the design of preventive interventions. One challenging problem in such analysis is that the form of behavior evidenced in reciprocal relations changes across the child's development. For example, the child and parent may influence each other steadily across development with the child's "problem" behavior influencing the parent's "problem" behavior and vice versa, but the parent's problem behavior changes from noncontingent harsh disciplinary practices in early childhood to poor monitoring and supervisory practices in early adolescence. After reviewing studies of the transactional model, Sameroff and Mackenzie (2003) concluded that "(p)roblems remain in the need to theoretically specify structural models and to combine analyses of transactions in the parent–child relationship with transactions in the broader social contexts" (p. 613).

A multisystem transactional model of the development of adolescent aggression toward female partners has been postulated by Capaldi, Dishion, Stoolmiller, and Yoerger (2001). Following from Patterson (1986), they proposed that early coercive parent–child interactions influence a child's aggressive behaviors and the selection of the child's peer group. The peer group then takes on an increasing socializing role during adolescence, locking the youth into a trajectory that started with earlier family interactions. In their empirical analyses, parental coercion predicted boys'

4

aggressive behavior, gravitation toward peer groups that engaged in hostile talk about women, and physical aggression toward a female romantic partner, in an escalating transaction.

Sameroff and Mackenzie (2003) have suggested that "(t)here is good reason to believe that the onset of substance use and abuse may follow a transactional socialization process similar to the one outlined by Patterson and others for aggression and conduct problems" (p. 623). They cited the need to add even more complexity by accounting for the role of the social ecology in moderating the relations between the child and others. Sameroff and Mackenzie (2003) further noted that part of the problem with empirical studies of complex transactional models is that statistical methods have been applied primarily to, at most, two relationships and three time points (e.g., parenting predicts child behavior, which mediates future parenting). Without explicit empirical testing, Wills and Yaeger (2003) concluded that "(t)he evidence favors a transactional model in which family factors have largely mediated effects on adolescent substance use through relations to adolescents' self-control, life events, and peer affiliations" (p. 222).

Recent conceptualizations of development of substance use behavior have capitalized on both transactional and dynamic systems theories. Masten, Faden, Zucker, and Spear (2008) called for models of underage drinking that incorporate principles of developmental psychopathology, especially person–environment interactions and transactions, multilevel analysis, and person as agent. They noted, "Underage drinking is a complex issue, deeply embedded in the developmental, multilevel, dynamic processes operating over time within and between individuals and their contexts" (p. S248). The metaphor of *cascades*, as in tumbling water that increases in speed and force as it is altered by, and alters, rocks in its path, captures some of the dynamic and transactional qualities of development that these theorists have proposed. Masten et al. (2005) were among the first to use the term "developmental cascade" to describe the relation between academic achievement and behavior problems in children across a 20-year period of development.

The current monograph represents one of the first attempts to broaden empirical tests of a transactional model to multiyear time points and relationships. We propose a dynamic cascade model, in which early ecological and child factors set in motion a chain of events that unfold, grow, and magnify over time into serious problem behavior in adolescence, in much the way that a stream meandering down a meadow joins other streams and gathers momentum and grows into a rushing rapid that cascades over rocks, carrying the rocks with it, albeit with various deflections from the rocks along the way. The rocks become part of the growing force that, by the end of the journey, leads to an outcome that in retrospect seems inevitable. In this effort, we attempt to provide an empirical, social–developmental realization of Waddington's (1962) germinal notion of an epigenetic landscape.

Our model involves transactional relations among the child, parents, and peers across development. Specifically, the model posits that early ecological and child risk factors make it difficult for a parent to parent effectively. Dysfunctional parenting, in turn, influences the young child to behave incompetently and disruptively upon school entry. This behavior pattern has an adverse effect on peers, who reject the child and increase conflict with him or her. These conflicts cause stress for the parent, which paradoxically leads the parent to withdraw from supervision, monitoring, and communication with the early-adolescent child just at a time when the child needs these parenting behaviors the most. In turn, the parent's withdrawal affords the youth the opportunity to associate in unfettered ways with deviant peers, which potentiates the onset of illicit substance use. We propose to test each of the hypotheses stipulated in this model with a novel application of partial least-squares (PLS) modeling. The result of this specific hypothesizing and empirical testing is a model that reduces a welter of correlations into a coherent dynamic developmental model.

DEVELOPMENTAL PATTERNS IN ADOLESCENT SUBSTANCE USE

By age 18, 72% of American adolescents report having tried alcohol, 55% report having been drunk, and 49% report using an illicit substance such as marijuana or inhalants (Johnston, O'Malley, Bachman, & Schulenberg, 2008). Plots of hazard rates by age-of-onset of these substances indicate that very few children initiate use before age 8. Risk of onset is particularly steep for each year between ages 10 and 18 and then declines sharply thereafter (Johnston et al., 2008; Kandel & Logan, 1984; Kandel & Yamaguchi, 1985).

These trajectories vary for different substances, but most substance users have begun use before the end of adolescence. Smoking almost always begins in adolescence: 89% of adult daily smokers began using cigarettes by or at age 18. In fact, 71% of adult smokers say that their smoking had become daily by adolescence (U.S. Department of Health and Human Services, 1994). Risk for alcohol consumption increases sharply in adolescence (Chassin, Flora, & King, 2004), precedes risk for marijuana use by several years (Kosterman et al., 2000), and declines more sharply after age 18 (Kandel & Yamaguchi, 1985). Cloninger (1987) described two types of alcoholism disorders: Type 1, called late-onset, begins in the mid-20s (although use begins in adolescence), and Type 2, called early-onset, begins in adolescence. Personality variables distinguish between these types (Cloninger, Sigvardsson, & Bohman, 1988). Donovan's (2007) review of the various surveys identified a group of 3–8% of youth who initiate alcohol consumption on at least a weekly basis at a very early age (before age 12). He highlighted this group for further inquiry and possible preventive intervention.

In some empirical studies, measures of consumption of alcohol, tobacco, and other drugs have been combined into a single construct called ATOD (e.g., Needle, Su, & Lavee, 1989; Newcomb & Bentler, 1988; Wills, Sandy, Yaeger, & Shinar, 2001) or weighted-persistent substance use (Loeber, Stouthamer-Loeber, & White, 1999), and have even been combined with a broader array of behaviors to form a "problem behavior syndrome" (e.g., Jessor & Jessor, 1977). In contrast, the different prevalence rates, life-course patterns, and legal consequences of each behavior suggest that developmental analyses might keep them distinct (e.g., Dishion, Capaldi, & Yoerger, 1999; Jackson, Hendrickson, Dickinson, & Levine, 1997; Kosterman et al., 2000; Masse & Tremblay, 1997). We assert that the extent to which a substance-use construct aggregates scores across tobacco, alcohol, and illicit substances, as well as age of use, will diminish the likelihood of discovering important developmental–ecological factors in substance-use onset. Although similar logic might suggest that distinctions should be made within the group of illicit substances, the high degree of overlap in use and the relatively low base rates of single-type users suggest merit in studying the group of any illicit substance users. The current study focuses exclusively on any illicit substance use (i.e., marijuana, cocaine, heroin, inhalants, and other illegal drugs) annually from age 12 to 18, allowing us to distinguish early versus later onset during adolescence.

EARLY VERSUS LATER ONSET OF ADOLESCENT SUBSTANCE USE

Several perspectives suggest the importance of distinguishing early from later onset of substance use, including different prevalence rates, different long-term outcomes, and possibly different etiologies. The nearly ubiquitous nature of late-teenage drinking implies that merely experimenting with this behavior in a senior high school cultural context of social drinking is not a strong predictor of adult problem outcomes, even though almost all adult alcoholics begin drinking before adulthood. As Clark and Winters (2002) concluded, "(E)xperimentation with alcohol, tobacco, and other drugs is part of the normal developmental trajectory for adolescents" (p. 1214). However, early initiation of drinking or illicit substance use (during elementary or middle school) may be especially diagnostic of later problem outcomes. The U.S. nationwide Monitoring the Future Study indicates that, by the eighth grade, 39% of youth report drinking alcohol and

19% report using marijuana (Johnston, O'Malley, Bachman, & Schulenberg, 2008). In French-speaking Montreal, Canada, by age 15 years, 48% of boys report being drunk in the past year and 31% report using some other drug (Masse & Tremblay, 1997). Donovan's (2007) review identified a group of 3–8% of youth who initiate alcohol use even earlier, before sixth grade. These lifetime prevalence rates indicate that onset of substance use grows across adolescence, with groups of very-early users, early users, and normative users.

In a different but related domain, consensus understanding of antisocial behavioral development distinguishes early-starting conduct problems from adolescence-initiated delinquency (Dodge, Coie, & Lynam, 2006; Dodge & Pettit, 2003; Moffitt, 1993; Patterson, Capaldi, & Bank, 1991). The former is hypothesized to be more serious, longer lasting, and impervious to treatment, whereas Moffitt (1993) has described the latter as socially normative.

The normativeness of high school drinking and substance use suggests that a similar distinction between early-onset substance use (which is initiated in a social context in which such behavior is deviant) and adolescence-onset substance use might be important. Although a sharp distinction by age of onset has not yet been formally applied to illicit substance use, empirical evidence indicates that the earlier one initiates substance use the graver the consequences. Early age of alcohol initiation is strongly linked to later alcohol misuse (Hawkins et al., 1997), progression to other drugs (Kandel, Yamaguchi, & Chen, 1992), lifetime alcoholism (Yu & Williford, 1992), and other problem behaviors (Gruber, DiClemente, Anderson, & Lodico, 1996; Robins & Przybeck, 1985). Likewise, early initiation of illicit substance use is a predictor of later use of other substances (Ellickson, Hays, & Bell, 1992), substance abuse (Kandel & Davies, 1992), and a variety of problem outcomes, including educational underachievement and unemployment (Newcomb & Bentler, 1988), antisocial behavior (van Kammen & Loeber, 1994), and general maladaptation in adulthood (Kandel, Davies, Karus, & Yamaguchi, 1986). Although later-onset illicit substance use is relatively normative, it is still costly and may also have origins in experience factors that could be avoided. Whether the experience factors differ for early versus later onset is not yet known. The current study included an age-of-onset parameter to test whether predictors of onset vary with age of onset.

UNDERSTANDING EARLY-ONSET SUBSTANCE USE

Whereas later adolescence-onset substance use has received relatively little attention, explaining early-onset substance use and identifying unique predictors of early- versus late-onset substance use are matters of great controversy. Cloninger (1986, 1987) has argued that early-onset alcohol use is due to an inherited personality pattern that consists of high novelty seeking, low harm avoidance, and low reward dependence (defined as responsiveness to social rewards and not as impulsive reward sensitivity). These characteristics reflect actions of neurally mediated behavioral activation, inhibition, and maintenance systems, respectively.

Evidence consistent with this theory is plentiful. In a sample of 431 Swedish males, these three personality dimensions were significantly related to early-onset alcoholism (Cloninger, Sigvardsson, & Bohman, 1988). Wills, Vaccaro, and McNamara (1994) found that these characteristics predicted early-onset cigarette smoking, alcohol use, and marijuana use. Pomerleau, Pomerleau, Flessland, and Basson (1992) found that novelty seeking and harm avoidance, but not reward dependence, were correlated with cigarette smoking in adulthood. Masse and Tremblay (1997) found that novelty seeking and harm avoidance, but not reward dependence, measured by teacher ratings at age 6 predicted self-reports of early-onset alcohol and marijuana use between ages 10 and 15 years. The theoretical thrust of these findings is that core personality characteristics are responsible for early-onset substance use. Implied is the assertion that environmental events exert little impact on substance-use development.

In contrast, Dishion, Capaldi, and Yoerger (1999) have offered a more ecological perspective. They suggest that features of the home, school, and neighborhood settings (such as stigmatization, victimization, behavioral norms, and economic resources) provide a context that leads to early behaviors (such as antisocial behavior, negative affect, and problematic temperament) that might appear as "inherent" child characteristics. The same settings were hypothesized to foster the development of substance use. Furthermore, Dishion et al. (1999) hypothesized and found that family management practices of harsh discipline and poor monitoring and peer experiences of social rejection and association with deviant friends have a direct impact on the development of early-onset marijuana use and partially mediate the effect of early context factors on marijuana use. Unfortunately, their measures of child characteristics were confounded in time with their measures of parenting, such that strong associations between a child's antisocial behavior at age 9 and early-onset substance use between ages 10 and 15 could not be interpreted definitively. They concluded that "both genetic and environmental theorists might endorse these findings as supportive" (p. 199). Furthermore, they could not distinguish (either in time or statistically) the separate impacts of family versus peer experiences on substance-use development. They ultimately aggregated all of these factors into a parsimonious but theoretically unsatisfying single construct that they called "childhood risk structure" that accounted for 34% of the variance in substance use. The current study offers time-specific measurement of key constructs in an ecological model in order to test the unique role of each factor.

REVIEW OF RISK FACTORS FOR YOUTH SUBSTANCE USE

The following brief review of the literature of the various types of risk factors provides a context for our proposed comprehensive model of the development of early-onset substance use. Emphasis is given to prospective studies and replicated findings. The review will appear more like a laundry list of risk factors than an integrated developmental story, and so the section following the review will weave the risk factors together into a developmental model.

Child Factors

Heritability has been posited as a driving force in problematic and early-onset substance use. The evidence is consistently supportive for genetic effects on alcoholism in males but not in females. Twin studies (Hrubec & Omenn, 1981) reveal higher concordance among male monozygotic twins than dyzogotic twins, and adoption studies (Cadoret, Cain, & Grove, 1980) indicate rates of alcoholism up to 27% for adopted sons of alcoholics compared with only 6% for adopted males without a biologic alcoholic parent. However, studies that include females have found no such effects (Murray & Stabenau, 1982), and studies evaluating genetic transmission of early-onset illicit substance use have yet to reveal consistent patterns (Hawkins, Catalano, & Miller, 1992).

Dick et al. (2006) have identified specific genes (e.g., GABRA2) that place adolescents at risk for substance-use problems, but they noted that genetic risk is confounded with risk for other conduct problems and probably represents a general genetic factor of deviance proneness. More likely than a direct genetic effect on illicit substance use is a genetic effect on cognitive and physiological factors that affect the development of a variety of deviant behaviors including substance use. A heterogeneous set of genes may be related to a heterogeneous set of cognitive biases toward immediate reward and sensation seeking as well as molecular markers of tolerance or susceptibility to addiction (Dick et al., 2006; Institute of Medicine, 1994; Nestler & Landsman, 2001; Tarter et al., 1999). Thus, a genetically informed developmental model of substance use might include measures of early conduct problems as precursors of later substance use and must wrestle with a possible common genetic cause.

But a common genetic cause does not rule out a role for environmental influences in determining which form of deviance occurs and in accounting for the link between early conduct problems and later substance use. Furthermore, more empirically striking than genetic main effects are gene–environment interaction effects (Dick et al., 2009) that indicate that genetic expression occurs only in the context of specific environments. The genetic findings mirror behavioral discoveries in adolescent developmental psychology: Life events shape the form of deviance that is expressed. This conceptualization suggests that heritable risk requires specific life experiences to potentiate and mediate the risk.

The complexity and ambiguity of mechanisms of heritable risk are highlighted in robust empirical findings that living with a parent who abuses alcohol or illicit substances increases risk of early-onset substance use (Merikangas et al., 1998; Weinberg & Glantz, 1999). Parental alcoholism (Cloninger, Bohman, Sigvardsson, & von Knorring, 1985; Goodwin, 1985) and substance use (Brook et al., 1990; Hops et al., 1990; Johnson, Schoutz, & Locke, 1984) substantially increase a child's likelihood of early-onset alcohol use (Chassin, Curran, Hussong, & Colder, 1996) and illicit substance use (Costello, Erkanli, Federman, & Angold, 1999). Dishion, Capaldi, and Yoerger (1999) followed 206 boys in the Oregon Youth Study and found that parental alcohol use and marijuana use (but not over-the-counter drug use) when the boys were in fourth grade significantly predicted boys' alcohol and marijuana use by age 15. Similarly, Kaplow et al. (2002) followed 387 kindergarten boys and girls from four geographic sites and found that parental substance use predicted children's substance use by age 12. Although parental substance use indexes an empirically important risk factor, the causal mechanism of this effect is unclear and could variously reflect genetic influences, a family context of psychopathology, or parental modeling of deviant behavior.

Whether markers of genetic risk or not, constitutionally endowed temperament and early behavior-problems constructs have been posited as child risk factors for alcohol and substance use (Tarter & Vanyukov, 1994). After reviewing the evidence from extant longitudinal studies of behavioral development, Zucker (2006a) noted, "This work, coming from six long term prospective studies carried out over the past quarter century, provides a remarkable convergence with the genetic literature in demonstrating that externalizing symptomatology appearing in early childhood is predictive of SUD (substance use disorder) outcomes some 15–20 years after the first appearance of the drug-nonspecific behavioral risk" (p. 616).

Two temperament factors derive from Gray's (1987) theory of neural control. A strong behavioral activation system is reflected in exhilaration that is activated by novel stimuli (high novelty seeking). The behavioral inhibition system adaptively heightens responsiveness to aversive stimuli, and a weak system will fail to facilitate the inhibitive behaviors that avoid harm (low harm avoidance). Zuckerman (1987) has found that novelty seeking (which he calls sensation seeking) is linked biochemically to low platelet monoamine oxidase activity, which is correlated with early-onset alcoholism (Tabakoff & Hoffmn, 1988). Cloninger et al. (1988), Pomerleau et al. (1992), and Wills et al. (1994) all found associations between both of these factors and substance use. Most impressively, Masse and Tremblay (1997) reported that these two factors assessed at age 6 predicted onset of alcohol and illicit substance use between 10 and 15 years of age.

Other related temperament factors, including high activity level, negative withdrawal responses to new stimuli, arrhythmicity, rigidity, and distractibility, have been found to be significantly correlated with adolescent substance use (Weinberg & Glantz, 1999; Wills, DuHammel, & Vaccaro, 1995; Windle, 1991). Using the Revised Dimensions of Temperament Survey (Windle & Lerner, 1986) and the Emotionality, Activity, and Sociability Inventory (Buss & Plomin, 1984), Wills et al. (2001) found that a temperament composite of high activity level and negative emotionality correlated significantly with a combined measure of self-reported ATOD use among sixth, seventh, and eighth graders surveyed in school. Because the substance use measure combined types of substances, it is not clear whether the temperament composite related significantly to illicit substance use. Likewise, prospective follow-up of 5-year-old children into young adulthood revealed that early difficult temperament, characterized by slow adaptability to change, negative mood, and withdrawal responses to new stimuli, predicted adolescent ATOD use (Lerner & Vicary, 1984).

Dishion et al. (1999) found that mothers' nine-item ratings of a child's "early difficulties" in the first 5 years of life (e.g., sleep problems, physical development problems) predicted later alcohol and marijuana use. In a major review, Zucker (2006b) concluded that a child factor of externalizing symptoms displayed early in life places a child at risk for later substance use problems, but this factor interacts and transacts with other factors across development to determine whether the form of externalizing disorder involves substance abuse or other behaviors.

In spite of the strong gender and race associations with externalizing behaviors (Dodge, Coie, & Lynam, 2006), and the strong associations between externalizing problems and substance use, substance use (particularly late-onset use) does not show similar associations with ethnicity and gender. Unlike studies of conduct problems (which find that African Americans are at greater risk than European Americans; Dodge et al., 2006), surveys indicate slightly lower rates of substance use among African American adolescents than European American adolescents (Costa, Jessor, & Turbin, 1999; Johnston, O'Malley, & Bachman, 1995; Maddahian, Newcomb, & Bentler, 1988), or no differences (Chilcoat & Anthony, 1996; Wills et al., 2001). In contrast, Kosterman et al. (2000) found higher rates among African American youth than European American youth. Kaplow et al.

(2002) found that African American children are at higher risk than European Americans for very early-onset (sixth grade) alcohol and substance use. It may be that minority ethnicity (and its environmental disadvantages) is correlated with early-onset substance use but not more normative use in adolescence.

Whether predictors of substance use vary across ethnic groups is a matter of debate, with some studies indicating that peer factors play a relatively stronger role in cigarette smoking for European Americans (Landrine et al., 1994), whereas family factors play a stronger role in illicit substance use for African Americans (Krohn & Thornberry, 1993). Bray, Adams, Getz, and McQueen (2003) found no ethnic group differences in the role of peers' behavior in adolescents' alcohol use, and Gottfredson and Koper (1996) found very few differences in risk factors for substance use among 981 African American and White 6th–10th graders.

Males appear to be at greater risk than females for early-onset alcohol and illicit substance use (Costello et al., 1999; Kaplow et al., 2002; Liu & Kaplan, 1996; Thomas, 1996) and for serious substance-use disorder that is comorbid with other psychiatric disorders (Kandel et al., 1997; Lewinsohn, Rohde, & Seeley, 1995). However, the differences tend to be so small that Armstrong and Costello (2002) concluded that "the similarities between the sexes have been more remarkable than the differences" (p. 1234). Recent data show that girls' use is almost equal to that of boys, particularly at younger ages (National Center on Addiction and Substance Abuse, 2003). Data from the National Household Survey on Drug Abuse show an increase in alcohol initiation among early adolescent girls (Substance Abuse and Mental Health Services Administration, 1997). In addition, while the age of first usage is getting younger for both boys and girls, it is dropping at a faster rate for girls. Three decades ago, initiation of alcohol use in the group of young teen girls ages 10–14 was only 7% but has grown in the last decade to 30.9%. This increase for young girls' initiation rates is compared with a relative increase from 20.2% to 35.4% for boys.

It was concluded that measures of gender, temperament, and early behavior problems are essential child risk factors for empirical analysis in the current study, but measures of later behavior problems probably confound genes and life experiences so much as to be less useful.

Early Family Social–Ecological Factors

Coexistent with child risk factors for early-onset illicit substance use is social–ecological factors within the family context during the child's early life. Although there is outdated evidence that high parental education and upper income levels are associated with slightly greater marijuana use among high school seniors (Bachman, Lloyd, & O'Malley, 1981; Zucker &

Harford, 1983), extreme economic poverty is also a risk factor for alcohol and illicit drug use (Robins & Ratcliff, 1979). More recently, Costa, Jessor, and Turbin (1999) and Dishion, Capaldi, and Yoerger (1999) found a negative association between family socioeconomic status and problem drinking in adolescence. Kaplow et al. (2002) found that children from the lowest socioeconomic-status group were at higher risk for very early-onset (before age 13) alcohol or substance use than other children.

In addition to family socioeconomic disadvantage, other early family contexts that have been demonstrated to enhance risk for early-onset substance use include being reared in a family missing a biological parent (Costa, Jessor, & Turbin, 1999), parental disorganization and emotional instability (Block, Block, & Keyes, 1988; Brook et al., 1990), and parental stress as indexed by child care problems, family medical conditions, unemployment, and the ratio of children to adults in the household (Dishion et al., 1999).

Early Parenting and Caregiving Factors

As found by Dishion et al. (1999), the development of early-onset substance use is more directly predicted by family interactions that a child experiences during his or her early years than the context into which that child is born. The ecological context might lead to family interactions that account for the impact of the context on development. The most-studied early parenting behavior is discipline style. Dishion et al. (1999) observed parent–child interaction at home at age 9 and indexed a poor-discipline factor that included nattering (ineffectual and annoying talking), abusive parenting (verbal attacks, physical strikes, and threats), and erratic discipline practices. This poor-discipline construct predicted boys' alcohol and illicit substance use by age 15.

At the extreme of harsh discipline is physical abuse. Child maltreatment, which encompasses physical abuse, neglect, and sexual abuse, has been found to pose risk for substance use, especially substance-use disorder (Kilpatrick et al., 2000; Widom, Ireland, & Glynn, 1995). Early sexual abuse enhances risk for substance-use problems in girls (Kendler et al., 2000) and boys (Clark, Lesnick, & Hegedus, 1997). Physical abuse in the absence of sexual abuse also poses enhanced risk for substance-use problems (Kaplan et al., 1998), although not as strongly. Distinct from a harsh discipline style are nonviolent discipline practices that involve verbal reasoning and discussion. Kaplow et al. (2002) found that reasoning and discussion styles of discipline protect children from early-onset substance use, and Kosterman et al. (2000) found that a proactive family management style protected children from subsequent marijuana use.

Yet another relevant early parent-interaction factor is warmth and involvement between parent and child. Kandel and Andrews (1987) and Penning and Barnes (1982) found that lack of maternal involvement with a child increases risk for substance use. Shedler and Block's (1990) direct observations of mothers' cold nonresponsiveness and lack of encouragement of their child at age 5 predicted frequent marijuana use in adolescence. Kaplow et al. (2002) found that parents' lack of involvement in their kindergarten child's education at school also predicted later substance use. Brook et al. (1990) reported a causal pathway in which early strong parent–child attachment led to the child's internalization of mainstream norms and values, which, in turn, led the child to associate with nondeviant peers and to nonuse of drugs.

Other early parenting behaviors that have been associated with the child's onset of illicit substance use include parental inconsistent permissiveness (Baumrind, 1983), mothers' unclear rules for child behavior (Brook et al., 1990), and lack of family rules about daily chores, homework, and so on (Costa, Jessor, & Turbin, 1999). Parental failure to discourage deviant behavior early in life (the inverse is sometimes labeled as parental approval for drug use, although few parents directly encourage substance use before age 15) has been associated with adolescent substance use in numerous studies (Barnes & Welte, 1986; Brook, Gordon, Whiteman, & Cohen, 1986; Hansen et al., 1987) that span multiple ethnic groups (Jessor, Donovan, & Windmer, 1980). Less direct early parenting behaviors that enhance risk for a child's early-onset substance use include their modeling of deviant behavior (see the findings regarding parental substance use noted above), including their modeling of marital discord (Simcha-Fagan, Gersten, & Langner, 1986) and their numerous marital transitions since the child's birth (Dishion et al., 1999).

Early Child Behavior Factors

The child's early behavior-problem levels most likely both reflect the genetically based child-factor contribution to later problems and grow from parenting practices (Collins, Maccoby, Steinberg, Hetherington, & Bornstein, 2000). Of all early child behaviors that have been examined in this context, aggression toward peers has been most consistently predictive of later substance use. Kellam, Ensminger, and Simon (1980) found that aggressive behavior in the first-grade classroom predicted later drug use, whereas shyness did not (unless coupled with aggressive behavior). Kaplow et al. (2002) reported a similar relation for first-grade aggressive behavior as indexed by parents' daily reports, and Dishion et al. (1999) found a similar relation for fourth-grade antisocial behavior. Supportive findings have been reported by Boyle et al. (1992), Lewis, Robins, and Rice (1985), and Reinherz et al. (2000), among others.

McMahon et al. (2000) examined the role of psychopathology assessed in kindergarten and 1st grade in predicting initiation of tobacco use in Grades 4–7. Discrete-time survival analyses indicated that children exhibiting psychopathology of one or more types (e.g., conduct disorder, attention-deficit hyperactivity disorder [ADHD]) show a two- to threefold increase in risk of onset of tobacco use by Grade 7. Both community studies (Armstrong & Costello, 2002) and clinical studies (Clark, Parker, & Lynch, 1999; Disney, Elkins, McGue, & Iacono, 1999) show that early disruptive behavior disorders temporally precede eventual early-onset substance use. In fact, of all child psychiatric disorders that have been linked to adolescent substance use, conduct disorder stands out as the most consistent and strongest marker of risk (Glantz & Leshner, 2000), so much so that Glantz (2002) has called for randomized trials of interventions to reduce conduct disorder as a test of substance-abuse prevention.

ADHD (Mannuza, Klein, Bessler, Malloy, & LaPadula, 1998) has also been linked to later substance-use problems, but this relation has been attributed to its comorbidity with conduct disorder. Farmer, Compton, Burns, and Robertson (2002) concluded that "ADHD may indirectly increase risk of substance use disorders by increasing risk for antisocial disorders" (p. 1267). Likewise, early medication treatment for ADHD has been correlated with early-onset substance use (Kaplow et al., 2002), but medication may be a risk factor simply because it marks the presence of ADHD.

Internalizing behaviors have also been correlated with substance-use problems in adolescence (Kandel et al., 1999) and may immediately precede substance use in the short term (Deykin, Buka, & Zeena, 1992), but little evidence exists that internalizing problems early in childhood mark risk for substance use. In fact, early anxiety and other internalizing symptoms in the absence of disruptive behavior may actually protect a child from later alcohol use (Kaplow, Curran, Angold, & Costello, 2001), substance use (Kaplow et al., 2002), and tobacco use (Costello et al., 1999), perhaps because internalizing behaviors may prevent a child from interaction with a peer group that exposes the child to substances and substance-use culture.

Early Peer Relations Factors

As important in substance-use development as the child's behavior toward others is the reaction of the peer group to that behavior. Kaplow et al. (2002) found that social rejection by the first-grade peer group, indexed by the social preference score (number of liking nominations minus number of disliking nominations), predicted very early-onset illicit substance use.

Likewise, Dishion, Capaldi, Spracklen, and Li (1995) used the same score collected in fourth grade and found that it predicted tobacco, alcohol, and marijuana use by age 15.

Transactional theory (Sameroff, 2009) suggests that features of the child's behavior toward peers during this period may lead to the peer group's reactions and may also be a response to peer group rejection, but in either case both the child's behavior and the peers' reactions have been found to be important markers of later substance use. Whether the peer group's reactions increment the prediction of later substance use beyond the child's behavior has not been tested sufficiently. Greene et al. (1997, 1999) found that early social impairment predicted later substance-use disorder even after controlling for conduct disorder, other psychiatric disorders, and social class.

Early social competence, indexed in various ways, has been a consistent protective factor in substance-use development, even after controlling for conduct problem behavior. Jackson et al. (1997) found that third- and fifth-grade children with low teacher-rated social competence (separate ratings of social skills, self-confidence, and academic abilities) were at least twice as likely to report early use of alcohol as children with high competence. Other measures of social competence that have uniquely predicted later substance use include social problem-solving deficits and hostile attributional biases measured by responses to hypothetical vignettes (Kaplow et al., 2002), poor behavioral self-control skills (Griffin, Botvin, Epstein, Doyle, & Diaz, 2000), and expectations and aspirations for success in life (Costa, Jessor, & Turbin, 1999; Newcomb & Felix-Ortiz, 1992).

The particular importance of social competence is highlighted by non-robust effects of two related constructs in predicting substance use: self-esteem and intelligence. Measures of self-esteem have yielded contradictory findings. Although Costa et al. (1999) found that low self-esteem marked risk for alcohol use, Dishion et al. (1999) found no such relation. Likewise, measures of intelligence are not consistently predictive of substance use. *High* scores on intelligence tests predicted earlier and more frequent use of alcohol in an inner city sample (Fleming, Kellam, & Brown, 1982); in contrast, *low* scores on the Wechsler Intelligence Scale for Children — Revised in first grade predicted earlier substance use in Kaplow et al.'s (2002) four-site sample. In their review, Hawkins, Catalano, and Miller (1992) concluded that "(t)he available evidence suggests that social adjustment is more important than academic performance in the early elementary grades in predicting later drug abuse" (p. 84).

Although intelligence is probably not predictive of substance use, social–behavioral factors that are related to schooling have been identified as risk factors for substance use, including a low degree of commitment to school (Johnston, O'Malley, & Bachman, 1985), disliking of school (Kelly &

Balch, 1971), academic underachievement (Dishion et al., 1999), and truancy (Gottfredson, 1988).

Parenting and Sociocultural Factors in Early Adolescence

As a child moves into early adolescence, parenting factors continue to mark risk for substance-use development, but the relevant parenting factors shift away from harsh discipline to overall supervision, monitoring, and control of the youth's sociocultural environment. Chilcoat and Anthony (1996) followed 926 8–10-year-old urban-dwelling children into adolescence and found that a 10-item child-report measure of parental supervision and monitoring predicted later marijuana, cocaine, and inhalant use. Furthermore, decreases in parental monitoring across time signaled a subsequent increase in risk of initiating illicit substance use. Parental knowledge of a child's whereabouts, activities, and friends has been found to predict ATOD initiation (Barnes, Reifman, Farrell, & Dintcheff, 2000; Dishion et al., 1995; Flannery, Vaszonyi, Torquati, & Fridrich, 1994; Fletcher, Darling, & Steinberg, 1995).

Numerous studies support the importance of parental monitoring in protecting early adolescents from moving toward substance use (Baumrind, 1985; Dielman, Butchart, Shope, & Miller, 1991; McCarthy & Anglin, 1990), although Dishion et al. (1999) were surprised that their measure of monitoring, which predicted tobacco use, did not reach significance for marijuana use.

Stattin and Kerr (2000; Kerr & Stattin, 2000) have called into question the importance of parental monitoring behavior by pointing out that monitoring knowledge is less an outcome of parents' monitoring behaviors than it is of unsolicited child disclosure. Eaton, Krueger, Johnson, McGue, and Iacono (2009) took this point a step further by finding that child personality characteristics account for the effect of monitoring knowledge on child outcomes. The distinction between monitoring as knowledge (of whereabouts, companions, etc.) and monitoring as process (through what means do parents acquire this information) is now widely accepted. Furthermore, the distinction between monitoring and control/supervision is crucial. Fletcher, Steinberg, and Williams-Wheeler (2004) distinguished among parental knowledge, monitoring, and control behaviors in a longitudinal study of 2,568 adolescents. Their measure of control/supervision consisted of six youth-reported items: (1) How late at night I can stay out; (2) Which friends I spend time with; (3) How I spend my money; (4) Whether or not I can drink alcohol; (5) How much time I spend with friends; and (6) When I can start dating. They found that even controlling for knowledge and child disclosure measures, parental control/supervision behaviors significantly incremented the prediction of future substance use.

It is possible that parental supervision is especially important in particular ecological settings, such as neighborhoods that provide ready access to drugs, or for particular children who are prone to deviance. Pettit, Bates, Dodge, and Meece (1999) found that parental supervision predicted adolescent aggressive behavior, but only in high-risk neighborhoods and only for high-risk children. Similarly, Beyers, Bates, Pettit, and Dodge (2003) found that the protective effect of parental monitoring was more striking for those living in neighborhoods that census data indicated are high in residential instability and, thus, likely to have fewer informal social controls on children.

Finally, quality of the parent–child relationship in early adolescence has been found to mark risk (Hundleby & Mercer, 1987). Hawkins et al. (1992) refer to "low bonding to family" as the critical construct in characterizing early adolescents who are at risk for becoming involved with illicit substances.

Adolescent Peer Relations Factors

In early adolescence and throughout puberty, rapid brain development renders youths especially vulnerable to the attraction of immediate rewards and sensational stimuli (Dahl & Spear, 2004). During this era of life, peers provide pressure to seek immediate gratification and offer exposure to sensational stimuli, including drugs. In addition, peers grow in influence as parents' influence wanes; thus, adolescent peer relations factors are strong predictors of substance-use initiation (Bogenschneider, Wu, Raffaelli, & Tsay, 1998). Like parenting, though, the important aspect of peer relations changes. The predictive factor shifts away from overall acceptance by the mainstream peer group to association with deviant peers (Dishion & Owen, 2002). Early-adolescent involvement with peers who display deviant behavior, especially substance use, is perhaps the strongest predictor of subsequent initiation of substance use (Hawkins et al., 1992), presumably through processes of peer norms, modeling, and pressure.

Of course, deviant behavior by an adolescent might lead that youth to gravitate toward deviant peers, which would indicate a selection factor rather than causal impact of association with deviant peers. However, Gatti, Tremblay, Vitaro, and McDuff (2005) found that deviant influences in gang membership during midadolescence (ages 14–16) facilitated substance use, even controlling for selection factors into gang membership.

Transactional effects and reciprocal influences are plausible. Bray, Adams, Getz, and McQueen (2003) found that tenuous efforts to individuate from parental influence may even accentuate peer influences on alcohol use in adolescence. Furthermore, they found that the tendency to affiliate with deviant peers and one's own alcohol use reciprocally influenced each other over time, suggesting a spiraling path toward deviance across Grades 7–9.

Allison et al. (1999) found that middle and high school peer-group norms regarding the frequency and acceptability of alcohol and drug use were significant predictors of individual alcohol and drug use. Both actual peer-group drug use and the individual's perception of peers' drug use were unique predictors, suggesting that both peer behaviors and the youth's beliefs about peers contribute to drug use. A related mechanism through which association with deviant peers may increase substance use may be social in nature. Dishion et al. (1999) suggest that "(s)moking may serve as a mechanism by which boys with troubled peer relations have commerce in a peer group ... One may hypothesize that early onset smoking is a peer adaptation and has functional use in the life of the at-risk youth" (p. 199). Supportive findings come from studies across a wide range of ethnic groups and geographic contexts (Brook et al., 1990; Elliott, Huizinga, & Ageton, 1985; Griffin et al., 2000; Jessor et al., 1980; Kandel & Andrews, 1987; Kosterman et al., 2000).

In spite of these strong correlations, the causal status of deviant-peer influence remains under debate. As noted, the relation between youths' own deviance and peers' deviance has been found to be reciprocal. Changes in peers' use of substances increase a child's risk for substance-use initiation, but a child's initiation of deviant behavior also influences the peer group (Curran, Stice, & Chassin, 1997). Second, gravitation toward deviant peers is predictable from earlier peer rejection and externalizing problems (Laird, Jordan, Dodge, Pettit, & Bates, 2001) and negative affectivity (Shoal & Giancola, 2003), suggesting that association with deviant peers might be epiphenomenal to substance-use development unless these factors are controlled. Third, strong relationships with one's parents have been found to buffer a child from the effects of associating with peers who are deviant (Brook et al., 1990). Finally, not all early adolescents are susceptible to peer influence, even in the context of association with deviant peers. Goodnight et al. (2006) found that adolescents who are low in characteristics of impulsivity/reward sensitivity are relatively less susceptible to peer influences on delinquent behavior. The concept of "resistance efficacy" has been introduced to understand moderation effects of deviant peer associations and has been targeted by prevention programs as a way to enhance resistance to substance use (Botvin, 1986).

Nonetheless, association with deviant peers who provide exposure to drugs, use drugs, and act as models for how to use drugs represents the most proximal pathway to onset of substance use in the proposed cascade model.

THEORETICAL AND EMPIRICAL INTEGRATION

Both the diversity and redundancy in a list of risk factors call for empirical and theoretical integration. Rutter and Garmezy (1983) proposed a risk-factor counting approach, which has been used successfully to optimize the number of predictor variables in empirical models. For example, Kaplow et al. (2002) used an array of variables to find that, although any single risk factor increased risk of adolescent substance use from < 10% (for zero risk factors) to 30%, a child with two risk factors had over 50% risk and a child with three risk factors had over 60% risk.

A counting of risk factors to predict later substance use is still devoid of developmental understanding. Theoretical integration is needed. Most multicomponent developmental theories have been articulated in temporally sequential fashion. Simons et al. (1988) have suggested a multistage social learning model that posits initial risk from parental modeling of substance abusing behaviors, through the child's experimentation, followed by peer-group reward for using substances, and further increases in substance use. Dishion, Capaldi, and Yoerger (1999) also suggest a multicomponent model that includes risk factors of ecological context, family management, and peer environment. Although these models are integrative, they do not account for the full diversity of risk factors reviewed here, they do not account for the different ways that parents and peers influence youth at different points in development, and they do not suggest reciprocal relations in an ongoing transaction between the youth and the social world. Furthermore, they have not been fully tested in longitudinal inquiry.

The approach taken by theorists in developmental psychopathology captures most accurately the series of ongoing transactional effects that describe how child risk factors influence the environment but are also shaped by the environment across time (Dahl & Spear, 2004; Steinberg et al., 2006; Masten et al., 2005). Following this tradition, we propose a dynamic, cascading, multistage, incremental, transactional social learning model that is depicted in Figure 1. This model integrates diverse risk factors in a sequential fashion that posits the manner in which risk factors build upon each other to lead to early-onset substance-use initiation in adolescence.

Other cascading models of social development have been posited recently, in outcome domains of internalizing symptoms (Obradovic & Masten, 2007), externalizing symptoms (Dodge, Greenberg, Malone, & the Conduct Problems Prevention Research Group, 2008), psychiatric disorders (Koot & Timmermans, 2007), and academic competence (Moilanen & Shaw, 2007). These models have some features in common with the current model, but none of the prior models spans as many socializing domains as the current formulation, nor do they utilize the data-analytic approaches that are used here. The current model is described in preliminary form by Dodge et al. (2006).

The model begins with child factors and family socioecological factors in very early life, including temperament as a child factor and demographics

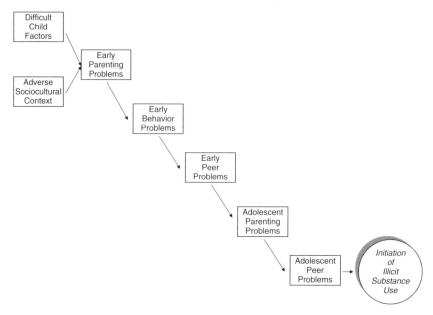

FIGURE 1.—A multistage transactional social learning model of substance-use development.

and socioeconomic status as ecological factors. The model posits that a child with a difficult temperament and a family history of substance use who is born into a family of poverty and stress, headed by a single, socially isolated, teenage, alcohol-using mother who gives birth following an unplanned pregnancy with medical complications, is at heightened risk for substance use 15 years later. Not all of these factors are necessary, of course. It is posited that these factors place a child empirically at risk for later use of substances. These factors tell us little about the mechanisms through which that development occurs, which is left to subsequent stages.

The next step of the model involves early parenting and caregiving. Following from McLoyd (1990), it is hypothesized that early child and ecological risk factors make it difficult for parents to manage their child effectively. Furthermore, it is hypothesized that inadequate parenting during these early years predicts later deviant behavior, including substance use. Specifically, the model posits that (1) negative parenting experiences in the first 5 years of life are predictable from temperament risk factors and adverse ecological contexts; (2) negative parenting experiences in the first 5 years of life increase a child's risk for adolescent substance use, above and beyond the risk imposed by previous child and family factors; and (3) these parenting factors partially mediate the effect of previous factors on substance-use development.

22

Thus, like other models of youth problem behaviors (e.g., Dodge, Pettit, & Bates, 1994a; Sampson & Laub, 1994), it is posited that risks induced by ecological–structural and child factors operate partially through their adverse effect on early caregiving. Children who are born into poverty and adversity are at risk to receive care that is characterized by harsh discipline (even physical abuse), a lack of positive parenting, interparental conflict, exposure to violence, and values that support deviant behavior, with a high rate of nonmaternal (but not paternal) child care. In turn, these caregiving experiences increase a child's risk for using drugs in adolescence and describe the processes through which early poverty and adversity cascade into later substance use.

The proposed model is a cascade, in that problems in early parenting, which partially emerge from previous child and context challenges, propel subsequent processes that account for the predictive effects of early factors. At the next step of the proposed model, children who have received deficient early parenting are likely to enter elementary school displaying aggressive conduct problems. The literature strongly supports the impact of early dysfunctional parenting on growth in aggressive behavior. Furthermore, early conduct problems are among the most robust predictors of adolescent substance use, especially early-onset use. It is hypothesized that the child's early conduct problems predict later substance use, are predicted from early parenting, and mediate the impact of early parenting on later use. The growing model thus moves from child and ecological factors at birth to early dysfunctional parenting to aggressive conduct problems at school entry and ultimately to adolescent substance use. But how do relatively conduct problems in first grade lead to substance use in adolescence?

Caprara, Dodge, Pastorelli, and Zelli (2007) have proposed a theory of how initial marginal deviations in a child can grow into larger problems and disorder over time, through processes of social feedback, self-cognition, and dynamic transactions with the peer and adult environment. A child's aggressive conduct problems often incite negative reactions in peers and teachers, specifically, social rejection by the classroom peer group, which reciprocally exacerbates the child's conduct problems (Dodge et al., 2003). Instead of reacting in a way that would bring the child's behavior back into the mainstream, peers paradoxically push a marginally deviant child toward greater deviance (Caprara, Dodge, Pastorelli, Zelli, & the Conduct Problems Prevention Research Group, 2006). One of the characteristics of dynamic cascade models is that each step of development offers an opportunity for the child or the environment to disrupt the cascade (as in a dam across a river) or to exacerbate the process (as in a waterfall).

It is hypothesized that the experience of peer rejection exacerbates the child's risk for later substance use, beyond the effect of behaviors that led to social rejection. The mechanisms of this impact probably include increases in negative affectivity, as well as reduced opportunity for positive peer influence, although these mechanisms are not empirically tested here. Nonetheless, it is hypothesized that peer social rejection partially accounts for the effect of conduct problems on later substance-use outcomes.

Beyond exacerbating conduct problems, how does peer conflict lead to substance use? Like other transactional models, this model posits that a child's peer relations, which have been influenced by the child's previous behavior and parenting patterns, will, in turn, predict later parenting patterns. Thus, the model posits reciprocal, transactional exchanges between parenting and peer relations. As the child moves into early adolescence, however, the key tasks of parenting change, and so the relevant features of parenting differ from the relevant features of parenting earlier in childhood. In early childhood when the parent's direct socializing influence is paramount, the key tasks of parenting are behavior management and teaching self-regulatory skills; in early adolescence, when the youth is surrounded by a myriad of other social influences, the key task becomes management of the youth's activities and exposure to other socializing forces.

The proposed model posits that social rejection in the conduct-problem child is likely to exacerbate conflict with his or her parents during the early adolescent years because of the trouble that peer conflict causes at school and in the neighborhood. Repeated peer fights and trouble, leading to parents' unwanted trips to the school, school suspensions, and perhaps disruptions at extracurricular activities and neighborhood centers, wear on parents over time. As a result, the parents become likely to give up attempts at socializing their child and to withdraw from monitoring and supervising their young teen, as Patterson, Reid, and Dishion (1992) have demonstrated empirically. Thus, it is hypothesized that previous child peer relations problems will predict a parental pattern of low monitoring and poor supervision.

It is further hypothesized that poor parental supervision will increase the child's risk for initiating substance use, beyond the risk from peer relations problems, and it is hypothesized that parental monitoring will partially mediate the effect of early peer experiences on subsequent substance use. But what is the interpersonal process through which this effect occurs?

Ironically, just at the developmental era when the high-risk child needs increased monitoring and supervision by parents, the high-risk youth is often left to roam the neighborhood during after-school and weekend hours with no one charting her or his whereabouts. So, the final step of the proposed model involves another set of reciprocal relations. It is hypothesized that adolescents whose parents do not supervise their behavior adequately are likely to gravitate toward deviant peer groups. Thus, adolescent parenting patterns, which had developed partially from earlier peer relations patterns, are hypothesized to influence another aspect of peer relations, association with deviant peer groups. The deviant peer group, in turn, exposes the youth to new deviant activities and culture, including illicit substances. Whether the motive is sensation seeking, self-medication, or group acceptance, the youth's ready access to drugs through the deviant peer group affords the opportunity that makes using drugs a high probability. Thus, it is hypothesized that low parental supervision will predict association with deviant peers. It is also hypothesized that deviant peer associations, in turn, will predict the onset of substance use, even after controlling for parental supervision. Finally, it is hypothesized that deviant peer associations will partially mediate the impact of adolescent parenting problems on later substance use.

The model incorporates the major risk factors at various developmental eras and ties them together in a theoretically sensible, although perhaps not obvious, manner. Each risk factor builds on previous risk factors by both mediating the impact of previous risk factors on later development and incrementing that risk through a new interpersonal process. The major players of parent, youth, and peers are always involved but in evolving ways that reflect the youth's stage of development. The combination of all risk factors provides a powerful empirical prediction of adolescent substance use and a plausible account of how these factors operate on the youth.

GENDER

Numerous studies have consistently found that males are at greater risk than females for both early-onset substance use (Bray, Adams, Getz, & McQueen, 2003; Kaplow et al., 2001) and later-onset substance use (Siebenbruner, Englund, Egeland, & Hudson, 2006). However, the literature is much less clear about gender-specific predictors of substance use. Gottfredson and Koper (1996) found little evidence to support gender specificity in a longitudinal study of 981 youth using measures of parental supervision, peer influence, and self-efficacy as predictors. All of these factors predicted frequency of drug use, and the strength of the relations did not vary across gender. We did not propose the developmental cascade model in a gender-specific manner. Nonetheless, in the current study we tested the hypothesis that models of prediction of substance-use trajectories would differ across gender groups.

EMPIRICAL HYPOTHESES

The model in Figure 1 suggests seven sets of hypotheses, each pertaining to one of the seven predictor domains for adolescent substance use outcomes. When possible, within each set, five noncompeting, complementary hypotheses were tested that followed similar logic:

Ha1: *Domain$_i$* will predict adolescent substance use.

Ha2: *Domain$_{i-1}$* will predict adolescent substance use.

Ha3: *Domain$_{i-1}$* will predict *domain$_i$*.

Ha4: *Domain$_i$* will mediate partially the impact of *domain$_{i-1}$* on adolescent substance use.

Ha5: *Domain$_i$* will increment the prediction of adolescent substance use beyond *domain$_{i-1}$*.

First, variables in a domain (*domain$_i$*) were hypothesized to predict adolescent substance use onset. Second, variables in the immediately antecedent domain, *domain$_{i-1}$*, were also hypothesized to predict adolescent substance use. Third, variables in *domain$_{i-1}$* were hypothesized to predict variables in *domain$_i$*. Fourth, variables in *domain$_i$* were hypothesized to mediate partially the impact of variables in *domain$_{i-1}$* on adolescent substance use. Fifth, variables in *domain$_i$* were hypothesized to increment the prediction of adolescent substance use beyond variables in *domain$_{i-1}$*.

Another five hypotheses within each set tested similar hypotheses but with *domain$_{i+1}$*, instead of adolescent substance use, as the outcome, as follows:

Hb1: *Domain$_i$* will predict *domain$_{i+1}$*.

Hb2: *Domain$_{i-1}$* will predict *domain$_{i+1}$*.

Hb3: *Domain$_{i-1}$* will predict *domain$_i$*.

Hb4: *Domain$_i$* will mediate partially the impact of *domain$_{i-1}$* on *domain$_{i+1}$*.

Hb5: *Domain$_i$* will increment the prediction of *domain$_{i+1}$* beyond *domain$_{i-1}$*.

As with Hypothesis a1, Hypothesis b1 states that variables in a domain (*domain$_i$*) would predict variables in a later domain, this time *domain$_{i+1}$*. Second, Hypothesis b2 states that variables in the immediately antecedent domain, *domain$_{i-1}$*, would also predict variables in *domain$_{i+1}$*. Hypothesis b3 is that variables in *domain$_{i-1}$* will predict variables in *domain$_i$*. This hypothesis is actually the same as Hypothesis a3 but is repeated for ease of following the process. Next, Hypothesis b4 states that variables in *domain$_i$* would mediate partially the impact of variables in *domain$_{i-1}$* on variables in

$domain_{i+1}$. Hypothesis b5 states that variables in $domain_i$ would provide an increment in the prediction of variables in $domain_{i+1}$ beyond variables in $domain_{i-1}$.

A final set of hypotheses addressed the full model simultaneously.

DATA ANALYTIC CHALLENGES

Historically, at least nine data analytic challenges have impeded testing the hypotheses listed above. These problems have been addressed in the current study through the application of contemporary methods and adherence to several decision rules.

The first challenge is that the "factors" (i.e., domains) in the proposed model are not hypothesized to be scales with highly correlated markers of a unitary underlying factor. With scales, it is assumed the measured indicators are caused by a single latent construct, so that the indicators are perfectly correlated with each other except for measurement error. Examples are scales of neuroticism and verbal intelligence. In contrast, an index is an aggregated sum of theoretically similar variables that are not presumed to be caused by a single latent construct or to be highly correlated with each other. Nonetheless, these variables are summed into an index because they are hypothesized to exert similar impact on other outcomes in a cumulative way. It is very plausible that variables might not be caused by the same construct but could still have similar impact on some outcome. One example is a stressful life events index. Although events such as a parent's death, loss of a job, and divorce are not assumed to be caused by the same source, or even significantly associated with each other, they have been found to exert similar adverse impact on one's health. Thus, it is justified to aggregate them into a single index.

Consider the current study's early parenting domain, which includes the variables nonmaternal child care, harsh discipline, positive parenting, and father involvement, among others. A major theoretical contribution to the field by Parke, Burks, Carson, Neville, and Boyum (1994) has been the discovery that various parenting variables are *not* indices of a single underlying construct. Instead, they are theoretically distinct and (relatively) empirically independent variables. Empirical studies validate this hypothesis. Pettit, Bates, and Dodge (1997) found that measures of positive parenting are empirically independent of measures of harsh discipline, and Bates et al. (1994) found that parents' child care decisions are only modestly associated with their disciplinary strategies. In the domain of later parenting, Pettit, Keiley, Laird, Bates, and Dodge (2007) found that parental monitoring is independent of discipline patterns. Laird, Pettit, Dodge, and Bates (2003) found that changes in parents' monitoring knowledge are only modestly related to parent–child relationship quality and discipline practice. Thus, variables in the parenting domain fit the model of an index better than that of a scale.

Kraemer (2008) has identified numerous problems with conducting mediational analyses in which constituent variables are treated as a scale when they violate the assumption of unity of the latent construct. Thus, it is neither theoretically nor statistically plausible to fit a single latent factor to this heterogeneous array. On the other hand, keeping every variable separate in data analysis would lead to an inefficient omnibus regression with 35 predictor variables, so the challenge is how to aggregate variables in a coherent way that retains their statistical and theoretical independence.

We identified PLS analysis (Chin, 1998) as a data-analytic approach, which is theoretically consistent with our hypothesized model. PLS is a variation of principal components analysis that results in a composite that is maximally related to some criterion. This composite is a weighted sum of observed scores and not a latent variable as in a factor analysis. This is a key distinction because PLS modeling allows theoretically related variables to be collated without the assumption that they are all indicators of a common source of variance, which is assumed in structural equation modeling (SEM). One of the implications is that correlations among the component variables need not be as high in order for the model to converge as would be necessary for a successful confirmatory factor model. Thus, standards for empirical correlations among variables within a domain can be appropriately relaxed.

Consider the domain of sociocultural risk, which in the current study includes family socioeconomic status, teenage pregnancy, and family stress (among others). SEM requires the assumption that one underlying construct *causes* all of these indicators, whereas PLS allows the constituent variables to be independently caused with relatively low intercorrelations. The assumptions of PLS more accurately represent the domains under inquiry in the present study. Although PLS has been used in the past to relate constructs to each other (e.g., Chin, 1998), the current study is innovative in using PLS in mediational analyses involving three constructs (i.e., a predictor, an outcome, and a mediator).

The second challenge is how to model both the occurrence and timing of onset (early or late) of the dichotomous outcome variable of substance use as a function of multiple predictor variables. Discrete-time survival analysis (Willett & Singer, 1993) is a flexible tool for modeling the timing of events in a panel design. The models can be manipulated to test specific hypotheses, such as changes in the hazards of onset over time.

The third challenge concerns the typically high stability of individual differences in behavioral variables, making detection and prediction of change difficult. Cole (2006) argued that the study of developmental transitions improves the testing of change (and processes in change) because the transition itself signifies relative instability. In the current study, we addressed this challenge by focusing measurement on two important developmental transitions, to school and to adolescence.

Four more challenges relate to the testing of mediation. Ideally, a test of mediation includes three time points with all three variables (predictor, mediator, and outcome) measured at all three points, in order to distinguish developmental influences from mere stability in behavior (Cole, 2006; Cole & Maxwell, 2003). However, some developmental phenomena involve emergent behaviors that are not measurable at all time points. Substance-use onset is such an emergent behavior. On the other hand, it may be that stability in the *pattern* or construct of behavior, rather than the form, characterizes development. An apparent emergent behavior such as substance use might simply represent continuity in a pattern of deviance whose form changes with environmental and developmental context. Little, Weaver, King, Liu, and Chassin (2008) have identified a robust association between a construct of "deviance proneness" and marijuana use. Because this correlation may vary with secular trends, gender, and other moderators, marijuana use is not merely an indicator of the construct but is consistently correlated with it. Thus, the fourth challenge is to control for variables that might indicate an underlying pattern of deviant behavior.

In the current study, the best indicators of a pattern of early deviant behavior were mother-rated infant temperament scores and early behavior-problem levels. Consideration was also given to controlling for recent behavior in addition to early behavior, in order to generate the tightest test possible of the impact of a predictor variable on an outcome. However, the hypotheses of the cascade model suggest that the pattern of behavior itself may be influenced by developmental transactions with the environment, and so a test of the impact of a predictor on an outcome must be careful not to include as a covariate an endogenous outcome variable that is itself actually influenced by the predictor variable.

Consider that an outcome O at T4 is being predicted from a predictor P at T2 and a mediator M at T3. At what time point should the "prior" level of O be measured? O at T1 represents the underlying construct of the outcome. O at T2 represents the underlying construct of O at T1 plus any environmentally induced change in O. Thus,

$$O_{T2} = O_{T1} + (O_{T2} - O_{T1}).$$

In this equation, the term $(O_{T2} - O_{T1})$ is entirely determined by environmental or intrapersonal variables at T2 and is by definition endogenous to the developmental process. If the test includes as a covariate the outcome variable at T2 or T3, then a true relation between the predictor and the outcome may be masked. In the current study, the initial level of an underlying construct of behavior problems, indexed by temperament and the T1 behavior problems score, was used as a covariate.

The fifth challenge is that conventional tests of mediation tend to be underpowered to detect indirect effects (MacKinnon, Lockwood, Hoffman, West, & Sheets, 2002a). Furthermore, they assume a normal distribution with symmetric confidence intervals, an assumption that rarely holds in mediation tests (Bollen & Stine, 1992). The current study uses indirect effects that were estimated as the product of the two component path co-efficients with an asymmetric empirical confidence interval that was derived by bootstrapping. This is the test that MacKinnon and colleagues recommend as apt to yield accurate significance tests.

The sixth challenge is that developmental transactional models such as the one posited here have historically been articulated at a more elaborate level than the level at which they have been tested. Models that have been described as multistep, sequential paths have been tested simply through multiple regression analyses with β coefficients, or, at best, as three-variable structural equation models. The tests used here map directly onto the level at which the full model has been articulated.

The seventh challenge concerns testing of moderation through inter-action effects within mediation models. Multiple-group analyses have been developed to examine gender specificity in predictive models, and they were used here.

The eighth challenge is a common one in prospective inquiry over a long period of time; sporadic missing data for individual variables often cumulate to compromise the data set under list-wise deletion. The solution is that missing data can be multiply imputed (Schafer, 1999), and this method was applied presently.

The final challenge is another common one in large long-term prospective studies, although it is rarely discussed. Because of the time and expense of collecting data, many variables are collected. Thus, a data set such as this one has many more variables than can possibly be utilized in any single report. Selection of variables for inclusion in constructs, and constructs for inclusion in model testing, necessarily has some arbitrariness that may seem flawed in retrospect. Sometimes investigators will arrive upon an optimal set of variables after multiple failed tests and will report the final set without reporting the previous failed tests. We followed a process of reviewing the literature, generating hypotheses, and then selecting variables and constructs based on these hypotheses, with the constraint that all variables must be measured in temporal sequence. That is, because the hypotheses are temporally based, all variables that are hypothesized to predict a later variable must be measured before the later variable. There is one

exception, which is that measurement of mother's lifetime alcohol use occurred after several variables that it is hypothesized to predict. Because we
had failed to measure this variable at Time 1 and yet it is so crucial to most
theories, we elected to retain it. Most importantly, though, we tested hypotheses with the a priori selected variable set even though we might have
been able to increase internal consistency of constructs and the strength of
cross-construct correlations by post hoc addition and deletion of items. We
do not doubt that stronger correlations could be found within this data set,
but we believe that our process provides a fair test of the hypothesized
model.

II. STUDY DESIGN AND METHODS

PARTICIPANTS

Participants were part of a multisite longitudinal study called the Child Development Project (see Dodge, Bates, & Pettit, 1990). The participants were recruited when the children registered for public kindergarten across two cohorts in 1987 or 1988 at each of three sites: Knoxville, TN; Nashville, TN; and Bloomington, IN. Within each site, about six schools that served families from a range of socioeconomic status (SES) groups were selected to participate, explicitly including schools in economically at-risk neighborhoods. Parents were approached at random during kindergarten preregistration and asked if they would participate in a longitudinal study of child development. Because approximately 15% of children at the targeted schools did not preregister, a corresponding number of participants were recruited on the first day of school or by letter or telephone. Of those asked, approximately 75% agreed to participate.

The sample consisted of 585 families at the first assessment (58% boys; 81% European American, 17% African American, 2% other). The Hollingshead (1979) index of families' SES indicated a wide range, from 11 to 66, with a mean in the low-middle class ($M = 39.59$, $SD = 13.96$). Follow-up assessments were conducted annually through Grade 12. Varying levels of missing data were found across measures. For the basic outcome measure of illicit substance use in adolescence, which is based on scores that are aggregated across indicators at Grades 7, 9, 10, 11, and 12, 87% of participants contributed at least one of the component measures. Higher percentages contributed to every other major domain of variable.

Of the original 585 families, 74% participated at the last time point in Grade 12. Participants with and without Grade 12 data did not differ significantly on any Time 1 demographic measures, except kindergarten SES. Participants who provided data in Grade 12 had slightly higher SES ($M = 40.38$, $SD = 14.25$) than participants who did not provide data in Grade 12, $M = 37.37$, $SD = 12.91$; $F(1, 567) = 5.17$, $p < .05$.

MEASURES

Early Child Risk Factors

Although we conceptualize these factors as beginning at birth, our first assessment occurred during the summer before children started kindergarten or within the first weeks of school, when in-depth interviews were conducted with mothers in their homes. The limits of this timing must be acknowledged. Five early child risk factors were measured within the context of these interviews either through mothers' direct reports or through interviewer ratings made following mothers' responses to open-ended questions (see Deater-Deckard, Dodge, Bates, & Pettit, 1998). During the initial home interview, mothers reported their child's *race* and *gender* and completed the Retrospective Infant Characteristics Questionnaire (Bates & Bayles, 1984; Bates, Freeland, & Lounsbury, 1979; Bates et al., 1998). This instrument asks the mother to report about her child's temperament at age 12 months, including items on negative emotionality and manageability, yielding a reliable score for *temperament risk* (9 items, $\alpha = .86$). In addition, mothers described the child's health during the prenatal through early postnatal period. Based on this description, interviewers then privately rated *medical complications* ($1 = healthy\ at\ birth$, $2 = minor\ or\ brief\ problems$, $3 = major\ health\ problems$).

Finally, the *mother's lifetime history of alcoholism* was assessed through the 13-item Short Michigan Alcoholism Screening Test (Selzer, Vinokur, & Van Rooijen, 1975) administered to mothers when the child was in the 11th grade. Examples of items include "Do friends or relatives think you are a normal drinker?" and "Have you ever gotten into trouble at work because of drinking?" Mothers responded *no* (coded as 0) or *yes* (coded as 1) to each question, and a total score was obtained by summing responses across items ($\alpha = .67$). The short-term stability of this instrument has been found to be over .90 (Teitelbaum & Carey, 2000), and the long-term stability of self-reported problems in alcohol use has been shown to be high. Hansell et al. (2008) found an average test–retest stability correlation of about .60 across an 11-year period in a sample of 1,158 adults, and this pattern has been replicated in multiple studies (e.g., Culverhouse et al., 2005). However, it must be noted that this instrument was collected many years after the child was an infant, and the stability of the score is not clear.

Sociocultural Risk Factors

Seven sociocultural risk factors were assessed during the same first session. *SES* was based on the Hollingshead (1979) Four-Factor Index of Social Status, which includes scores for mother and father education and occupation. Families were coded as headed by a *single mother* ($0 = married\ or\ living$

33

with another adult, 1 = single mother), and a ratio of children to adults (log transformed) in the household was computed on the basis of mothers' reports of who lived in the household at the time of the initial assessment. Mothers' teenage pregnancy was based on their age at the time of their first pregnancy (0 = younger than 19 years, 1 = 19 years or older). Planfulness of the pregnancy with the target child was based on mothers' reports (1 = planned, 2 = unplanned but under discussion, 3 = unplanned but accepted, 4 = unplanned, unprepared). Mothers were asked whether they had experienced each of 15 major stressors from the time the child was 1 year old through the year preceding the interview and again in the last year. A family stress scale was created by summing responses to these 30 questions (each rated 0 = had not occurred, 1 = had occurred; see Dodge, Pettit, & Bates, 1994b). Maternal social isolation was coded by the interviewer following a series of questions regarding mothers' social contact and who was available to help them in times of need (1 = very well supported, 5 = very isolated).

Early Parenting and Caregiving

During the prekindergarten interviews, eight parenting and caregiving variables were assessed. Mothers reported the extensiveness of nonmaternal child care in the child's first year of life (0 = none to 6 = more than 30 hours per week for more than 7 months) and from the age of 1 year through the time of the interview when the child was approximately 5 years (0 = none to 4 = more than 20 hours per week; see Bates et al., 1994). Scores were standardized and averaged across these time periods. Mothers reported the biological father's involvement and support (0 = no help to 4 = good help). Child exposure to interparental conflict was coded after mothers answered questions about the child's exposure to arguments, conflicts, and violence between parents (1 = none to 5 = physical more than once). Child exposure to family and neighborhood violence was coded after mothers answered questions about the kinds of violence the child was exposed to inside and outside the home (1 = none to 5 = physical more than once).

Following a series of questions about who disciplined the child, how the child was disciplined, whether physical punishment was used, and whether the child had been disciplined severely enough to be hurt or require medical treatment, interviewers rated the extent to which the child experienced harsh discipline (1 = nonrestrictive to 5 = severe, strict, often physical discipline). Interviewers also rated whether the child had experienced physical abuse (1 = definitely not to 5 = authorities involved). Positive parenting was assessed through interviewer ratings of mothers' reports on the Concerns and Constraints Questionnaire (see Pettit, Bates, & Dodge, 1997), a series of questions about what mothers would do to prevent their own child from behaving in particular ways in response to five hypothetical vignettes

34

depicting child misbehavior (1 = *do nothing, is unpreventable*, to 5 = *preventable, anticipatory, situation-specific*). This score is internally consistent across items (α = .70) and modestly correlated with directly observed warmth between mother and child in a home visit (r = .22) (Pettit, Bates, & Dodge, 1997). Finally, *mothers' support of aggression* was assessed through the Culture Questionnaire (Dodge et al., 1994b), a 15-item measure that asked mothers to endorse items such as "I wouldn't mind if my child got a reputation as the toughest kid in school" (1 = *definitely disagree* to 7 = *definitely agree*).

Early Child Behavior Problems

Children's kindergarten teachers completed the 113-item Teacher Report Form of the Child Behavior Checklist (Achenbach & Edelbrock, 1986). Items were summed as raw scores to create separate scales reflecting *internalizing* and *externalizing* behavior problems.

Early Peer Relations

Three early peer relations variables were assessed. Sociometric nominations were made by children's peers annually from kindergarten through third grade. Children whose parents consented for them to participate (at least 75% of the children in each classroom) were presented with pictures (for kindergarten and first graders) or names (for second and third graders) of their classmates and were asked to nominate up to three classmates they liked the most (LM) and liked the least (LL; see Harrist, Zaia, Bates, Dodge, & Pettit, 1997). A kindergarten *social preference* score was created by taking the standardized difference between the standardized LM and the standardized LL ratings (see Coie, Dodge, & Coppotelli, 1982). Scores were standardized within classroom to control for variability in classroom size. A dichotomous rating of *peer rejection in kindergarten* was determined by social preference scores < -1, standardized LM scores < 0, and standardized LL scores > 0 (see Coie & Dodge, 1983). The *number of years rejected* reflected a sum of the number of years from kindergarten through third grade the child was rejected by their peers.

Adolescent Parenting Risk Factors

At age 11, a measure of *mother-reported parental supervision* was created by averaging nine items (α = .71; see Pettit, Bates, Dodge, & Meece, 1999), which were adapted from other measures of parental supervision (Brown, Mounts, Lamborn, & Steinberg, 1993; Capaldi & Patterson, 1989; Dishion, Patterson, Stoolmiller, & Skinner, 1991; Fletcher, Steinberg, & Wheeler-Williams, 2004). Using a 1–5 scale, mothers were asked to rate how much they knew about the adolescent's friends and activities, how difficult it was to

35

track their adolescent's whereabouts, and the likelihood of adult supervision at the homes of the adolescent's friends when their child was in the sixth grade. In the seventh grade, a measure of *adolescent-reported parental supervision* was created by averaging five items ($\alpha = .42$) that asked adolescents how much their parents really know about and direct who their friends are, how they spend their money, where they are after school, where they are at night, and what they do with free time ($1 = don't know$, $2 = know a little$, $3 = know a lot$).

Adolescent Peer Relations and Peer Sociocultural Risk Factors

Eight variables assessed adolescent peer relations and context. When adolescents were in the sixth grade, their mothers answered six questions about *neighborhood safety* adapted from the Self-Care Checklist (see Pettit et al., 1999; Posner & Vandell, 1994). Responses ($1 = very safe$ to $6 = very unsafe$) were averaged to create a scale ($\alpha = .90$) reflecting mothers' overall appraisal of the safety of the neighborhood, their safety coming home and being home alone, and their children's safety playing inside and outside the home. Mothers were also asked to think about the two peers their child spent the most time with after school. For each of those peers, mothers rated (a) whether they drink alcohol or use drugs and (b) whether they smoke cigarettes ($1 = never or hardly ever$, $2 = occasionally or sometimes$, $3 = very often or always$). The four items (two for each peer) were averaged to create a scale reflecting *mother-reported peer drug use* ($\alpha = .72$). A scale reflecting child-reported peer drug use in sixth grade was created by averaging six items ($\alpha = .48$) comparable to those asked of their mothers with the exception of separately asking about alcohol use and other drug use.

When adolescents were in the seventh grade, a scale reflecting *peer group drug use* was created by averaging adolescents' reports on three items ($\alpha = .76$) regarding how often their peers smoke cigarettes, drink beer or wine, and use illegal drugs ($1 = never$ to $5 = very often$). A scale reflecting *peer-group deviance* was created by averaging five items ($\alpha = .74$) regarding how often the peers get in trouble at school, get in fights with other children, use bad language, lie to adults, and like to do things that make the adolescent scared or uncomfortable ($1 = never$ to $5 = very often$; see Dishion et al., 1991; Laird, Pettit, Dodge, & Bates, 1999). A scale reflecting *best friend deviance* was created by averaging five items ($\alpha = .69$) modified from the peer group deviance items described above to refer to whether the best friend engages in deviant behaviors ($0 = not true$, $1 = somewhat/sometimes true$, $2 = very/often true$; see Dishion et al., 1991; Laird et al., 1999).

Adolescents' *susceptibility to peer pressure* in seventh grade was measured using the Doing Things with Your Friends interview, which presents adolescents with 12 hypothetical situations and asks what they would do in

36

each. For example, adolescents were presented with the scenario "One day after supper, you and a couple of your best friends meet at school. No one is around and your friends decide that you should all write on the walls of the school with chalk. You don't think it is a good idea, but your friends tell you to do it anyway. What would you *really* do?" Adolescents first decided whether they would write on the school walls and then how certain they were about that decision (1–6 scale). Across situations, responses were reverse coded as needed so that higher scores reflect greater susceptibility to peer pressure. Items were averaged to create a scale ($\alpha = .72$).

Adolescents' seventh-grade teacher was asked to complete a series of questionnaires. Because most children had multiple teachers, school personnel (usually the principal or school secretary) were asked to nominate the teacher most familiar with the adolescent to complete the measures. The teacher rated whether the student's peer group or best friend was tough, dangerous to be with, rebellious, and drug/alcohol using (1 = *lowest 5%*, 2 = *lower 30%*, 3 = *middle 30%*, 4 = *higher 30%*, 5 = *highest 5%*). The four items were averaged to create a scale of *teacher-reported peer deviance* ($\alpha = .84$).

Adolescent Substance Use in Grades 7–12

When adolescents were in the seventh grade, they were asked how many times in the last year they (a) smoked marijuana and (b) used other drugs. Each item was rated on an 8-point scale (0 = *never*, 1 = *once or twice*, 2 = *once every 2–3 months*, 3 = *once a month*, 4 = *once every 2–3 weeks*, 5 = *once a week*, 6 = *2–3 times a week*, 7 = *once a day*). In 9th and 10th grades, adolescents rated how often they used illegal drugs on a 5-point scale (1 = *I never do this*, 2 = *I do this once in a while*, 3 = *I sometimes do this*, 4 = *I do this fairly often*, 5 = *I do this very often*). In 11th and 12th grades, adolescents indicated for each item whether they had huffed or inhaled a substance in the past 12 months and whether they had ever smoked marijuana, tried cocaine or crack, tried LSD or heroin, or tried any other way to get high (0 = *no*, 1 = *yes*).

We considered whether to construct separate variables for marijuana use and all-other-substances use. However, the overlap in self-reports of lifetime use of these two substances was very high, $\chi^2(419) = 95.4$, $p < .001$. By Grade 12, of the 266 adolescents who had reported never using marijuana, only 6 (2.3%) had reported using another substance. Also, in Grades 9 and 10, participants were not asked to report separately for each substance. Therefore, these measures were combined to create a dichotomous indicator in each year of *illicit substance use* (i.e., use of inhalants, marijuana, or other illegal drugs). The dichotomous (any use vs. no use) form of this variable was selected to yield a comparable indicator across years, given the variability in the measurement forms.

III. SUBSTANCE-USE PATTERNS AND CORRELATIONS AMONG VARIABLES

The purposes of this chapter are to provide an overview of how various data-analytic issues were managed, the empirical pattern of onset of substance use across the adolescent years, and the bivariate correlations among variables. The issues in data analyses were raised in the introduction at a general level and are taken up here in detail. The pattern of substance-use onset across years was expected to follow rapid, nonlinear growth between the grade levels of 7 and 12. Presentation of the bivariate correlations provides a preliminary examination of the research questions in this study, as well as information that may be necessary to assess the model testing in subsequent chapters.

RESULTS

Analysis Overview

Missing Data

Missing data rates varied by measure (see Table 1). Among the predictor variables, the median rate was 4.0%; rates were higher for adolescent self-reports (25.0–26.5%) and particularly for mother's report of neighborhood safety (56.9%) and teacher's report of peer deviance (46.3%). Missing data rates for the self-report substance-use variables ranged from 22.0% (11th grade illegal drug use) to 30.1% (10th grade illegal drug use). Missing data were imputed using NORM v.2.03 (Schafer, 1999). Thirty imputations were generated, sufficient to yield good efficiency for the degree of missing information reflected in most analyses; previous analyses with 10 imputations resulted in unacceptably low estimates of degrees of freedom for parameter tests. Estimates from multiply imputed data sets are unbiased under missing at random (MAR) but are slightly inefficient depending on

TABLE 1

MISSING DATA PROPORTIONS FOR EACH VARIABLE

Early child risk factors	
African American	—
Male	—
Temperamental risk factors	.048
Medical complications	.024
Mother's alcohol use	.274
Early sociocultural risk factors	
SES	.027
Single mother	0
Adult–child ratio (log)	.056
Teen pregnancy	0
Unplanned pregnancy	.022
Family stress	.089
Social isolation	.015
Early parenting and caregiving risk factors	
Nonmaternal child care	.039
Father's involvement	.193
Interparental conflict	.192
Exposure to family/neighborhood violence	.041
Harsh discipline	.015
Physical abuse	.017
Positive parenting	.032
Support of aggression	.046
Early behavior problems	
Internalizing behavior problems	.019
Externalizing behavior problems	.019
Early peer experience risk factors	
Social preference	.032
Peer rejection	0
Years rejected	.007
Adolescent parenting	
Parental supervision (mother report)	.205
Parental supervision (adolescent report)	.263
Adolescent peer and context risk factors	
Neighborhood safety	.569
Peer drug use (mother report)	.251
Peer drug use (adolescent report)	.250
Peer group deviance	.263
Peer group drug use	.265
Best friend deviance	.263
Susceptibility to peer pressure	.280
Peer deviance (teacher report)	.463
Substance use	
Grade 7 marijuana use	.270
Grade 7 other illegal drug use	.272
Grade 9 illegal drug use	.284
Grade 10 illegal drug use	.301
Grade 11 marijuana use	.232

Table 1. (Contd.)

Grade 11 inhalant use	.224
Grade 11 cocaine/crack use	.220
Grade 11 LSD/heroin use	.220
Grade 11 other illegal drug use	.224
Grade 12 marijuana use	.282
Grade 12 inhalant use	.279
Grade 12 cocaine/crack use	.279
Grade 12 LSD/heroin use	.280
Grade 12 other illegal drug use	.287

the proportion of missing information (not the proportion of missing data). With 30 imputations, multiple imputations (MI) is 98% efficient with 50% missing information. The imputation data set included the 37 predictor variables (recoded as needed; race was coded as African American, yes/no); 22 dichotomized self-report substance-use indicators; and additional variables included to support the MAR assumption, including parent and teacher reports of substance use, parent and teacher reports of internalizing and externalizing behavior at different years, and academic performance from standardized tests. Diagnostic plots indicated no difficulties in the imputation process. In particular, there was no excess autocorrelation between statistics from consecutive imputations, indicating that the imputations were effectively independent, random draws from the distributions.

NORM uses Markov chain Monte Carlo estimation for continuous variables. For categorical variables, generated values were rounded to the nearest legitimate response; for continuous variables, the range of generated values was truncated to match the possible legitimate score distribution.

Analyses

Weights for variables in each domain were computed through partial least-squares (PLS) analysis of imputed data using PROC PLS in SAS v.9.1 (SAS Institute, 2003). Parameter estimates and standard errors were generated from the analyses of imputed data using PROC MIANALYZE in SAS v.9.1 (SAS Institute, 2003) for the survival analyses, and Mplus v.3.12 (Muthén & Muthén, 2002) for the mediation analyses, both of which use standard formulae to combine results (Rubin, 1987). Note that the degrees of freedom for tests of parameter estimates based on MI are not simple functions of sample size but rather depend on the between- and within-imputation variance estimates; they can be interpreted as a general guide to precision of estimation. The degrees of freedom are not readily available from Mplus.

We adopted the following rules for reporting of statistical effects. We report all tests of hypothesized effects, whether or not they yield significant

TABLE 2

ILLICIT SUBSTANCE USE REPORT FREQUENCIES, BY GRADE

Grade	Rate
7	.052
9	.146
10	.220
11	.432
12	.513

Note. $N = 585$. Tabled values are proportions of sample reporting the behavior in or by each study year.

effects. Effects at the $p < .05$ level and lower are reported as significant. Effects between $p < .05$ and $< .10$ are reported as marginally significant, and all other effects are reported as nonsignificant. All nonhypothesized effects that are statistically significant at the $p < .05$ level are reported, and all other tests are not reported.

Substance-Use Rates

Table 2 displays the proportions of positive reports for illicit substance use throughout the study period. Figure 2 depicts the cumulative hazard rate for ever-using illicit substances, which indicates rapid nonlinear growth in substance-use onset during the early adolescent period. By Grade 12, the lifetime-use rate is .513, which is almost identical to contemporaneous nationwide estimates generated by the Monitoring the Future Study at that time (Johnston, O'Malley, & Bachman, 2002).

Table 3 lists means and standard deviations for all 35 predictor variables and provides correlations among them. Correlations among variables within a domain were generally positive and modest in magnitude.

Table 4 lists the correlations between each of the predictors (and their within-domain composites) and substance use at each year, as well as a cumulative indicator of substance use by Grade 12. Most of the predictor variables were positively correlated with substance use at one or more time points, including the cumulative "ever" variable, although the magnitude of association was generally modest.

Model Testing Strategy

Overview

Analyses that are described in each of the following chapters followed a general template to test hypotheses and alternate models. First, each of the variables in a class was tested independently for prediction of the onset of

41

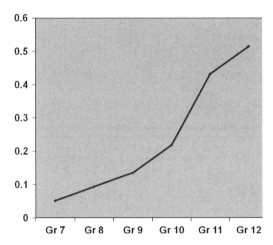

FIGURE 2.—Cumulative hazard from illicit substance use across adolescence (Grade 8 imputed).

substance use, using discrete-time survival analysis, and then the set of variables in the class was tested as a group in a multiple predictor model. Both the hazard for substance use and the timing of that hazard (as early—i.e., by the seventh grade—or later) were tested. Second, the predictability of a variable block was tested as a function of the temporally precedent block of variables. Third, the variable block was tested as a potential mediator of the relations between the temporally precedent block and the substance-use outcome.

Bivariate Prediction

Relations between each of the predictors and each of the substance-use variables were modeled using discrete-time survival analysis (Willett & Singer, 1993). In this strategy, the hazard function for the outcome variable (i.e., the log-odds of "failing to survive," or initiating substance use) is modeled at the baseline, where the predictor variable or variables are equal to zero. This is an estimate of the baseline odds of failure at each time point for a subject who has not failed before that time. Given this baseline, the hazard ratio is the proportional increase in odds of failure associated with a unit increase in the predictor. A hazard ratio exceeding 1 indicates an increased chance of failure with increases in the value of the predictor, identifying a risk factor; a predictor with a hazard ratio <1 is associated with reduced risk. Thus, for example, a hazard ratio of 1.18 associated with standardized scores on interparental conflict indicates that respondents

TABLE 3

MEANS, STANDARD DEVIATIONS, AND CORRELATIONS FOR PREDICTOR VARIABLES

Variable	1	2	3	4	5	6	7	8	9	10	11	12	13	14	15	16	17	18
1. African American	1.00																	
2. Male	-.03	1.00																
3. Temperamental risk	.07	.02	1.00															
4. Medical complications	.06	.01	.02	1.00														
5. Mother's alcohol use	.04	.01	.11	.07	1.00													
6. SES	-.40	.06	.00	-.04	-.07	1.00												
7. Single mother	.32	-.08	-.03	.02	.07	-.35	1.00											
8. Adult–child ratio (log)	.23	-.04	-.01	.07	.05	-.22	.37	1.00										
9. Teen pregnancy	.31	-.03	.01	.00	-.01	-.27	.20	.19	1.00									
10. Unplanned pregnancy	.15	-.05	-.06	-.03	.07	-.27	.21	.05	.09	1.00								
11. Family stress	-.04	-.01	.07	.02	.08	-.11	.24	.08	-.02	.11	1.00							
12. Social isolation	.14	-.05	-.05	.07	.04	-.27	.13	.09	.10	.12	.03	1.00						
13. Nonmaternal child care	.01	.04	.02	-.02	.02	.08	.08	-.08	-.01	.03	.14	-.13	1.00					
14. Father's involvement	-.27	.09	.05	-.04	-.08	.33	-.54	-.26	-.11	-.21	-.18	-.25	.01	1.00				
15. Interparental conflict	.19	.00	.03	.04	.08	-.33	.29	.10	.17	.07	.31	.20	.03	-.33	1.00			
16. Exposure to violence	.29	.00	.06	.09	.09	-.30	.25	.15	.16	.19	.16	.15	.00	-.27	.29	1.00		
17. Harsh discipline	.19	.10	.12	.08	.01	-.28	.09	.10	.07	.11	.11	.16	-.01	-.17	.32	.22	1.00	
18. Physical abuse	.19	.04	.08	.04	.01	-.37	.27	.13	.06	.23	.23	.16	.02	-.23	.42	.30	.55	1.00
19. Positive parenting	-.10	.01	.02	.01	-.14	.20	-.07	-.02	-.07	-.11	.04	-.14	.06	.16	-.03	-.04	-.07	-.06
20. Support of aggression	.17	.10	-.01	.00	.04	-.32	.11	.07	.09	.12	.06	.13	.00	-.11	.22	.13	.19	.20
21. Internalizing behavior problems	.04	-.02	-.01	.00	.07	-.15	.08	-.02	-.01	.08	-.05	.07	-.15	-.08	.00	.00	-.01	.12
22. Externalizing behavior problems	.10	-.04	.00	.01	.12	-.26	.21	.03	.10	.16	.04	.08	.13	-.19	.11	.06	.17	.22
23. Social preference	-.09	-.17	-.04	.00	-.04	.13	-.08	.05	-.12	-.09	-.08	-.04	.16	.10	-.11	-.08	-.15	-.19
24. Peer rejection	-.01	.10	.02	.06	.02	-.11	.02	-.05	.05	.08	.07	.08	.07	-.07	.11	.03	.15	.20
25. Years rejected	.06	.08	.04	.09	.07	-.18	.15	.00	.06	.12	.04	.10	.10	-.17	.15	.10	.17	.25
26. Parental supervision (mother report)	-.27	-.10	-.08	.04	-.04	.27	-.17	-.11	-.20	-.03	.02	-.15	-.01	.13	-.28	-.07	-.20	-.22

Table 3. (Contd.)

Variable	1	2	3	4	5	6	7	8	9	10	11	12	13	14	15	16	17	18
27. Parental supervision (adolescent report)	-.07	-.06	-.06	.02	-.01	.04	-.10	-.10	-.15	-.03	-.02	-.05	-.11	.09	-.11	-.11	-.15	-.08
28. Neighborhood safety	.31	-.09	.08	.01	-.02	-.28	.22	.17	.15	.12	.02	.14	.04	-.22	.14	.17	.19	.20
29. Peer drug use (mother report)	-.02	-.01	.02	.08	.06	-.10	.06	.03	.00	-.04	.05	.03	.02	-.08	.07	.06	.02	.02
30. Peer drug use (adolescent report)	-.01	.06	.09	.00	-.04	-.09	.09	.04	.10	-.01	.10	.00	.04	-.03	.08	.07	.07	.14
31. Peer group deviance	.14	.08	.00	.07	.03	-.17	.08	.02	.09	.05	.02	.11	.11	-.06	.06	.11	.06	.10
32. Peer group drug use	-.06	-.05	.05	-.04	.05	-.06	.03	.00	-.01	.06	.06	.08	.02	-.09	.05	-.02	.04	.06
33. Best friend deviance	.09	.15	.01	.04	.02	-.21	.13	.04	.03	.10	.02	.08	.05	-.09	.15	.13	.08	.15
34. Susceptibility to peer pressure	-.05	.19	-.02	.05	.03	.05	.01	.03	-.08	-.03	.10	.02	.09	-.04	.11	-.01	.05	.05
35. Peer deviance (teacher report)	.18	.09	.09	-.06	.04	-.34	.22	.11	.13	.17	.07	.12	-.04	-.13	.14	.20	.10	.23
M	.17	.52	3.30	1.28	0.68	39.58	.24	.19	.07	2.11	7.99	2.90	.00	2.85	2.21	1.75	2.68	1.54
SD	.37	.50	0.95	0.54	1.18	13.96	.42	.48	.26	1.13	4.25	0.96	.79	1.24	0.98	1.07	0.88	0.64
	19	20	21	22	23	24	25	26	27	28	29	30	31	32	33	34	35	

1. African American
2. Male
3. Difficult temperament
4. Medical complications
5. Mother's alcohol use
6. SES
7. Single mother
8. Adult–child ratio (log)
9. Teen pregnancy
10. Unplanned pregnancy
11. Family stress

Table 3. (Contd.)

	19	20	21	22	23	24	25	26	27	28	29	30	31	32	33	34	35
12. Social isolation																	
13. Nonmaternal child care																	
14. Father's involvement																	
15. Interparental conflict																	
16. Exposure to violence																	
17. Harsh discipline																	
18. Physical abuse																	
19. Positive parenting	1.00																
20. Support of aggression	−.19	1.00															
21. Internalizing behavior problems	−.07	.02	1.00														
22. Externalizing behavior problems	−.12	.11	.23	1.00													
23. Social preference	.01	−.07	−.15	−.34	1.00												
24. Peer rejection	.02	.07	.09	.26	−.62	1.00											
25. Years rejected	−.02	.08	.03	.34	−.54	.67	1.00										
26. Parental supervision (mother report)	.12	−.14	.04	−.15	.19	−.09	−.17	1.00									
27. Parental supervision (adolescent report)	.04	−.04	−.07	−.08	.11	−.04	−.03	.20	1.00								
28. Neighborhood safety	−.05	.07	.08	.11	−.06	.00	.04	−.23	−.15	1.00							
29. Peer drug use (mother report)	−.02	.02	.03	.08	−.03	−.01	.04	−.08	−.06	.13	1.00						
30. Peer drug use (adolescent report)	−.06	.15	.04	.08	−.07	.04	.02	−.12	−.10	−.02	.06	1.00					
31. Peer group deviance	−.07	.07	.01	.20	−.12	.08	.07	−.29	−.36	.22	.08	.04	1.00				
32. Peer group drug use	−.08	.00	.05	.11	.00	.03	.02	−.15	−.25	.02	.04	.07	.43	1.00			
33. Best friend deviance	−.05	.11	.05	.14	−.13	.08	.13	−.33	−.25	.18	.08	.06	.58	.26	1.00		
34. Susceptibility to peer pressure	−.01	.10	−.01	.10	−.04	.06	.01	−.12	−.34	.04	.02	.01	.43	.32	.39	1.00	
35. Peer deviance (teacher report)	−.12	.14	.08	.27	−.19	.17	.15	−.25	−.02	.05	.04	.09	.28	.20	.25	.09	1.00
M	3.31	2.98	48.00	50.24	.96	.31	.77	.37	.26	2.03	1.04	1.02	1.87	1.18	.32	2.57	1.73
SD	0.66	0.60	9.41	9.32	.96	.31	.77	.26	.13	0.89	0.13	0.68	0.68	0.42	.33	0.78	0.88

45

TABLE 4

BIVARIATE CORRELATIONS BETWEEN PREDICTOR VARIABLES AND SUBSTANCE USE

	Illicit Substance Use					
Predictor	Grade 7	Grade 9	Grade 10	Grade 11	Grade 12	Ever Use by Grade 12
Early child risk factors						
Race (African American)	.00	−.03	.00	−.02	−.04	.02
Gender (male)	.06	−.06	−.08	.01	.06	.00
Temperamental risk	.02	−.02	−.03	−.11	−.02	−.06
Medical complications	.00	.00	−.05	.00	.04	.02
Mother's alcohol use	.00	−.01	.00	−.02	.00	−.01
Composite	.03	.01	.03	.14	.06	.11
Early sociocultural context risk factors						
SES	−0.8	−.02	−.02	−.05	−.02	−.09
Single mother	.09	.06	.11	.07	.03	.09
Adult–child ratio (log)	.01	.03	.04	.08	.04	.07
Teen pregnancy	.02	.01	.12	.13	.02	.11
Unplanned pregnancy	.04	.00	.07	−.03	.01	.05
Family stress	.04	.10	.12	.09	.10	.08
Social isolation	.02	.00	−.06	.02	.02	.05
Composite	.09	.06	.13	.13	.07	.16
Early parenting and caregiving risk factors						
Nonmaternal child care	.03	.06	.02	.11	.09	.11
Father's involvement	−.06	−.03	−.01	−.08	−.04	−.10
Interparental conflict	.05	.08	.05	.10	.08	.11
Exposure to violence	.02	.01	−.01	−.03	−.07	−.02
Harsh discipline	.04	.04	−.05	−.02	.04	.04
Physical abuse	.11	.04	.01	.01	.02	.05
Positive parenting	.00	.00	.00	.00	.01	−.03
Support of aggression	.06	.01	.00	.08	.10	.09
Composite	.10	.08	.03	.14	.13	.18
Early behavior problems						
Internalizing behavior problems	.02	−.05	−.06	−.03	−.02	−.03
Externalizing behavior problems	.08	.07	.07	.14	.14	.15
Composite	.08	.08	.08	.14	.15	.16
Early peer experience risk factors						
Social preference	−.04	−.04	−.05	−.09	−.12	−.13
Peer rejection	.06	.05	.02	.06	.13	.11
Years rejected	.04	.04	.00	.03	.05	.06
Composite	.05	.05	.03	.08	.13	.13
Adolescent parenting risk factors						
Parental supervision (mother report)	−.09	−.14	−.09	−.10	−.13	−.17
Parental supervision (adolescent report)	−.13	−.09	−.08	−.13	−.12	−.16
Composite	.14	.15	.11	.15	.16	.21

Table 4. (Contd.)

	Illicit Substance Use					
Predictor	Grade 7	Grade 9	Grade 10	Grade 11	Grade 12	Ever Use by Grade 12
Adolescent peer and social context risk factors						
Neighborhood safety	.03	.01	− .02	− .06	− .07	.03
Peer drug use (mother report)	.12	.00	.03	.03	.04	.02
Peer drug use (adolescent report)	.14	.00	− .02	.11	.11	.10
Peer group deviance	.22	.16	.09	.17	.20	.24
Peer group drug use	.25	.23	.09	.12	.12	.15
Best friend deviance	.24	.12	.12	.19	.16	.21
Susceptibility to peer pressure	.24	.23	.21	.28	.25	.28
Peer deviance (teacher report)	.17	.06	.09	.06	.11	.13
Composite	.35	.24	.18	.28	.28	.33

Note. $N = 585$. Thresholds for significance vary.

who are 1 *SD* above the mean on that predictor show an 18% greater likelihood, relative to the mean, of beginning illicit substance use at any time point, given no use at previous time points.

In traditional proportional-hazards models, this change in risk due to the predictor is assumed to be equal across time. However, many of the predictors in the current models might be expected to have differential impact between early-onset substance use and later onset. Therefore, an interaction with time of substance-use measurement was incorporated, allowing a different hazard ratio at seventh grade (the earliest available) versus the subsequent years (assumed to be equal to each other); this allowed for differential prediction of early versus late onset.

Multivariate Prediction

The second stage of prediction modeling focused on effects of groups of predictors, with the ultimate aim being to identify sequential effects of different predictors as the constructs develop across time. The predictor variables were identified as comprising seven blocks. Each block was tested as a set of predictors in a survival model for illicit substance use. Interactions with time of onset were not included. This was a post hoc decision made to simplify the analyses when preliminary results showed few interactions with time (except for those predictors measured at early adolescence, which tended to show stronger relations with early—i.e., nearly contemporane-

47

ous—onset of substance use). Additionally, the unique contribution of each block was tested in a model with all previous blocks included.

Sequential Analysis

Issues of timing are implicit in the variable block construction, with attendant questions of causal sequence. That is, we hypothesize that the influence of child and sociocultural factors on substance-use onset is mediated, at least in part, by early parenting variables. Each chapter, beginning with Chapter V, includes a test of the hypothesis of mediation—mediation of the effects from the prior chapter by those from the current chapter. Because the relations of interest are between global assessments of "early child risk," "early parenting risk," and so forth, composites of the variables in each block were created. The common factor model, by which the relations among variables in a cluster are a result of a common source of variance, is not appropriate for most of the variable blocks considered here—sex and race, for example, do not share a common cause, nor are they correlated, but they might represent related sources of prediction for the outcome. Instead, composites were created by PLS modeling. PLS, in the same family of methods as principal component analysis, can be used to create variates that maximize the predictive utility between groups of variables (for an overview, see Chin, 1998). PLS models can also reflect relations among the latent variables, but current software does not permit integration with the survival aspect of the current hypotheses.

Each of the variable clusters was separately modeled in a PLS analysis with substance use by Grade 12 as the sole outcome variable (analyses used PROC PLS in SAS v8.2). This modeling resulted in composites of the variables in the clusters that were weighted to relate to the substance-use outcome. Table 4 displays correlations between each of these composites and the substance-use indicators. The correlations among the seven composite variates are presented in Table 5.

For each test of mediation, the composite scores for the earlier block and the intervening block were entered into a simple structural equation model with time of substance-use onset as the outcome; this model is saturated. Models were estimated in Mplus v.3.12 (Muthén & Muthén, 2002). The earlier block score was modeled as predicting the intervening block as well as having a direct effect on the outcome; the intervening block score predicted the outcome only. The outcome was modeled as an ordinal variable of time of onset. Although the version of Mplus used does have the facility to estimate discrete-time survival models, those models cannot also incorporate structural relations among the predictors. Treating the outcome as ordinal (in Mplus models, a continuous variable with discrete

48

TABLE 5

CORRELATIONS AMONG PREDICTOR COMPOSITES

Composite	1	2	3	4	5	6	7
1. Early child risk factors	1.00						
2. Early sociocultural context risk factors	0.04	1.00					
3. Early parenting risk factors	0.09	0.50	1.00				
4. Early behavior problems	0.08	0.22	0.27	1.00			
5. Early peer experience risk factors	0.06	0.14	0.23	0.33	1.00		
6. Adolescent parenting risk factors	−0.02	0.26	0.28	0.14	0.18	1.00	
7. Adolescent peer and context risk factors	0.03	0.16	0.21	0.22	0.15	0.45	1.00

Note. $N = 585$. Thresholds for significance vary.

measurement) avoided some of the more severe distortions imposed by rendering survival into a single variable. Tests of mediation were based on the empirical distribution of $\alpha\beta/\sigma_{\alpha\beta}$, where α is the effect of the exogenous variable on the mediator and β is the effect of the mediator on the outcome, as generated by MacKinnon, Lockwood, Hoffman, West, and Sheets (2002a). Examination of the online table of the empirical cumulative frequency distribution of $\alpha\beta/\sigma_{\alpha\beta}$ in the presence of no mediated effect suggests that a critical ratio of magnitude >0.96 is sufficient for statistical significance, $p < .05$ (MacKinnon et al., 2002b).

DISCUSSION

The pattern of rapid growth in onset of substance use across the Grades 7–12 is consistent with the annual cross-sectional reports by Monitoring the Future (Johnston, O'Malley, & Bachman, 1999, 2002; Johnston et al., 2008). The current report following two cohorts prospectively across time extends this literature by eliminating the plausible alternative of cohort effects that was possible in past cross-sectional studies. The adolescent period is characterized by rapid changes and nonlinear growth in problem behavior.

The pattern of modest positive correlations among variables within a domain indicates a problem for the identification of single latent constructs because convergence on a latent construct would be difficult. As a solution, the pattern indicates support for the use of PLS analysis because large within-domain correlations among variables are not required.

The pattern of multiple significant but modest positive correlations between predictor variables and substance-use onset suggests that the risk factors identified here perform in ways that are consistent with the past literature and that efficient ways of aggregating variables are necessary to understand substance-use development.

Missing data patterns, means and distributions of variables, and cross-variable correlations support the next steps of hypothesis testing.

IV. EARLY CHILD AND SOCIOCULTURAL FACTORS

At birth and in the first several years of life, both child characteristics and sociocultural context factors may indicate long-term risk for adolescent substance use by setting into motion a chain of life experiences that eventually becomes the dynamic cascade. Although the literature suggests many possible variables, we selected five child factors to represent this domain. Beyond race and gender (which are not empirically supported robust predictors but are included anyway because of their obvious identification value and possible value in interaction with other variables), the literature suggests that temperament may predict substance-use onset. Following Wills et al. (2001), we used a temperament composite variable from mother reports. Because medical complications at birth have been associated with later temperamental impulsivity, which is in turn a risk factor for substance use, we adopted this variable. Finally, because of the consistency of findings of genetic variables as risk factors (Dick et al., 2006), we followed Dishion, Capaldi, and Yoerger (1999) and used mother's reported alcohol use as a proxy for inherited risk.

Family sociocultural disadvantage and stress at or near the time of birth have also marked risk of later substance use (Dishion et al., 1999), and so we adopted seven empirically supported risk variables to represent this domain. Because Kaplow et al. (2002) found that lowest socioeconomic-status (SES) children were at relatively high risk for very early-onset (before age 13) substance use, we used the Hollingshead (1979) indicator of status. Following the finding by Costa, Jessor, and Turbin (1999) that children reared in a single-parent family are at risk for substance use, we measured this variable. We adopted the variable used by Dishion et al. (1999) of the ratio of children to adults in the household as a measure of family stress, in addition to parent reports of the number of stressful life events in the first 5 years of the child's life. Because parents who are not ready to parent may be at disadvantage, we used indicators for teen pregnancy and unplanned pregnancy. Finally, we used parent reports of social isolation.

51

METHOD

The participants are described above, as well as all measures. The first two hypotheses asserted the prediction of adolescent substance use from child factors and from sociocultural factors:

H1a: The set of early child risk factors will predict adolescent substance use.

H1b: The set of early sociocultural risk factors will predict adolescent substance use.

RESULTS

The early child risk factors and the sociocultural risk factors were taken as separate predictor clusters, with no temporal ordering assumed between them. They are treated separately in this chapter.

Early Child Risk Factors

The seven risk factors, taken as a set, were tested as a predictor of the onset of illicit substance use. There was no significant overall prediction, $F(7, 3573) < 1$, thus rejecting Hypothesis 1a. Each of the seven predictors in this cluster was also tested independently in relation to the onset of illicit substance use. None of the predictors was significantly related to onset, nor were there any significant interactions between time of measurement and the predictors. Parameter estimates and test statistics are presented in Table 6.

TABLE 6

SUBSTANCE-USE ONSET PREDICTION FROM EACH CHILD RISK FACTOR

Predictor	Hazard Ratio (95% CI)	t	df	p
Race (African American)	.05 (−.10, .19)	<1	486	ns
Gender (male)	−.01 (−.15, .13)	<1	577	ns
Temperamental risk	−.11 (−.28, .06)	1.30	946	ns
Medical complications	.02 (−.12, .15)	<1	1055	ns
Mother's alcohol use	−.02 (−.18, .14)	<1	219	ns

Note. $N = 585$. Tabled values are hazard ratios per standard deviation change in predictor.

TABLE 7

SUBSTANCE-USE ONSET PREDICTION FROM EACH SOCIOCULTURAL RISK FACTOR

Predictor	Hazard Ratio (95% CI)	t	df	p
SES	0.86 (0.75, 0.99)	2.18	1213	.029
Single mother[a]	1.50 (1.10, 2.04)	2.56	1218	.010
Adult–child ratio (log)	1.12 (0.96, 1.30)	1.48	376	ns
Teen pregnancy[a]	2.00 (1.19, 3.36)	2.63	316	.009
Unplanned pregnancy	1.08 (0.94, 1.23)	1.09	1362	ns
Family stress	1.16 (1.01, 1.33)	2.12	594	.034
Social isolation	1.05 (0.91, 1.17)	<1	653	ns

Note. $N = 585$. Tabled values are hazard ratios per standard deviation change in predictor, or unit change for categorical variables (marked).
[a]Categorical.

Early Sociocultural Risk Factors

The set of seven sociocultural risk factors was tested as a predictor of the onset of illicit substance use. The set significantly predicted substance use, $F(7, 4269) = 2.27$, $p < .03$, supporting Hypothesis 1b. Each of the seven predictors in this cluster was also tested independently in relation to onset of illicit substance use. Parameter estimates and test statistics are presented in Table 7. As indicated in that table, occurrence of substance use in adolescence was significantly predicted by low SES, being reared by a single mother, being born to a teenage mother, and by high early family stress.

None of the tests for interactions with time of measurement was statistically significant, $ps > .05$. In the model with all predictor variables entered, only mother's teen pregnancy contributed significant unique prediction of substance use, $HR = 1.80$, 95% CI: 1.04, 3.09, $t(354) = 2.12$, $p = .034$, all other $ps > .09$.

Finally, the seven child predictors and seven sociocultural factors were tested in combination. In this model, the child factors yielded no significant overall prediction, $F(7, 547) = 1.01$, ns; the sociocultural factors taken as a set continued to show significant unique prediction even when the set of child factors was controlled, $F(7, 4218) = 2.56$, $p < .02$.

DISCUSSION

The findings point to specific early sociocultural factors around the time of birth and in the first several years of life that place a child at risk for illicit substance use 12–17 years later in adolescence. Children who are born to teenage mothers, single mothers, families experiencing stress, and low-SES families are at heightened risk. The findings are in accord with the growing literature on social–ecological risk factors for substance use and add uniquely to this literature by improving the methodology of inquiry, clarifying the markers of risk and providing hypotheses regarding the mechanisms of this risk.

These results join Costa, Jessor, and Turbin's (1999) finding that emphasizes the heightened risk for substance use associated with family disadvantage, especially low SES. The findings add uniquely to the field in several ways. First, they point to the role of socioeconomic disadvantage before kindergarten (in addition to adolescence). This finding indicates that high-risk children can be identified early in life and that processes of the development of illicit substance use might be set into motion at a young age.

Second, the findings broaden the array of risk variables to factors that are correlated with low SES, including factors that had been overlooked or poorly measured in past research. Early measures of maternal age, psychosocial stress, and marital structure bring enhanced methodological rigor, and thus greater confidence, to the findings that these factors mark risk for substance use a decade into the future. Furthermore, modeling analyses indicate that SES is merely a marker of these other variables that more directly indicate risk, especially being born to a teenage mother.

The findings are also clear that the risk accruing from these family ecological factors cannot be accounted for by child factors such as ethnicity, temperament risk, maternal history of alcohol use, or medical complications at birth. In fact, the lack of prediction from child factors was surprising. Although substance use may cross generations, the absence of a direct relation between maternal alcohol use and youth substance use is important. This result joins Windle's (2000) finding that parental history of alcohol use is not as important as either sibling or peer use or parents' socializing behaviors and Brody, Ge, Katz, and Arias's (2000) finding that parental norms and standards for youth alcohol use may be more important than parental alcohol use history in predicting youth alcohol use. Of course, it is plausible that improved precision in measuring child factors would lead to the detection of significant associations.

V. EARLY PARENTING FACTORS

The findings above indicate that risk for adolescent substance use can be detected in early life from family sociocultural factors, but they do not describe the processes through which risk is exerted. We hypothesized that risk processes begin to operate through early-life parenting behavior. Stress, diversion of attention away from socialization and toward urgent goals of providing shelter and sustenance, lack of social support, and lack of opportunities to enhance parenting skills all may contribute to the parenting difficulties faced by mothers living in disadvantaged circumstances. These are the problems faced by single teen mothers, and they may render these mothers ill equipped to parent adequately during the child's first 5 years of life. Numerous studies provide a rationale for this hypothesis, albeit with child conduct problems as the outcome. McLoyd (1990) proposed that family economic disadvantage exerts indirect effects on child conduct problem outcomes through more direct effects on making it difficult to parent effectively. Sampson and Laub (1994) reanalyzed the Glueck data set to conclude that the effect of low socioeconomic status (SES) on juvenile delinquency could be accounted for by its effects on parenting inadequacy. Dodge, Pettit, and Bates (1994a) also found that low SES predicts child aggressive behavior and that this relation is statistically accounted for by the effects of low SES on parental harsh discipline patterns, which, in turn, more directly led to child aggressive behavior problems.

We sought to extend this work by testing a similar process with adolescent substance use as the outcome. Specifically, the hypotheses were tested that early family social–ecological factors would predict parenting difficulties during the first 5 years of life, especially regarding discipline practices. In turn, these parenting difficulties, whether they arise out of social–cultural adversity or not, place a child at heightened risk for adolescent substance use. Furthermore, the hypothesis was tested that early parenting difficulties account for the effect of social–ecological adversity on adolescent outcomes.

The proposed model does not posit a direct path from parenting behaviors to substance-use outcomes, however. The empirical findings described above point toward child conduct problems as a proximal outcome of dysfunctional parenting. Therefore, we also tested the hypotheses that early family sociocultural factors would predict child conduct problems and that early parenting dysfunction would predict child conduct problem outcomes and would mediate the impact of family sociocultural factors on conduct problems.

Thus, these hypotheses assert the role of early dysfunctional parenting in predicting, mediating, and incrementing risk for both adolescent substance use and early child conduct problems. The first five hypotheses address the prediction of substance use, and the second five hypotheses address the prediction of early child conduct problems:

H2a1: The set of early dysfunctional parenting factors will predict adolescent substance use.

H2a2: The sets of early child and sociocultural factors will predict adolescent substance use. (This hypothesis is redundant with previously tested Hypotheses 1a and 1b.)

H2a3: The sets of early child and sociocultural factors will predict early dysfunctional parenting.

H2a4: The set of early dysfunctional parenting factors will at least partially mediate the effect of child and sociocultural factors on adolescent substance use.

H2a5: The set of early dysfunctional parenting factors will increment the prediction of adolescent substance use beyond the level predicted by child and sociocultural factors.

H2b1: The early dysfunctional parenting variables will predict early child conduct problems.

H2b2: The set of early child and sociocultural factors will predict early child conduct problems.

H2b3: The set of early child and sociocultural factors will predict early dysfunctional parenting (already tested as Hypothesis 2a3 above).

H2b4: The set of early dysfunctional parenting factors will partially mediate the effect of child and sociocultural factors on early conduct problems.

H2b5: The set of early dysfunctional parenting factors will increment the prediction of early conduct problems beyond the
level predicted by child and sociocultural factors.

RESULTS

Prediction of Substance Use From Early Parenting Problems

The nine early parent risk factors, taken as a set, significantly predicted
onset of illicit substance use, $F(9, 4348) = 2.03$, $p = .033$, supporting Hypothesis 2a1. Each of the nine predictors in this cluster was tested independently in relation to onset of illicit substance use. Four of the predictors were
significantly related to onset, $p < .05$. As shown in Table 8, substance use was
significantly predicted from early nonmaternal child care, lack of father
involvement, high interparental conflict, and parents' support for the use of
aggression in problem solving. None of the predictors significantly interacted with time of onset. In the model with all early parenting variables
entered, only nonmaternal childcare showed significant unique prediction,
$HR = 1.19$, 95% CI: 1.03, 1.37, $t(794) = 2.43$, $p = .015$ (all other ps, ns).

Early Parenting as Mediator of the Relation Between Child/Sociocultural Factors and Substance Use

The early parenting risk composite score was tested as a mediator in
separate models for each of the child and sociocultural variable blocks. For
the model with early child risk factors, the relation between the early child
risk composite and substance-use onset (Hypothesis 2a2) was tested in the
previous chapter. The relation between the early child risk composite

TABLE 8

SUBSTANCE-USE ONSET PREDICTION FROM EACH EARLY PARENTING RISK FACTOR

Predictor	Hazard Ratio (95% CI)	t	df	p
Nonmaternal child care	1.19 (1.04, 1.36)	2.48	984	.013
Father's involvement	0.85 (0.74, 0.99)	2.15	390	.032
Interparental conflict	1.19 (1.03, 1.38)	2.38	351	.018
Exposure to violence	0.97 (0.84, 1.12)	<1	591	ns
Harsh discipline	1.05 (0.92, 1.20)	<1	1050	ns
Physical abuse	1.10 (0.97, 1.25)	1.43	1911	ns
Positive parenting	0.96 (0.93, 1.10)	<1	519	ns
Support of aggression	1.16 (1.01, 1.33)	2.12	930	.035

Note. $N = 585$. Tabled values are hazard ratios per standard deviation change in predictor.

and the early parenting risk composite was not significant, $b = .12$, $SE = .12$, est./$SE = 1.02$, ns, thus not supporting the first part of Hypothesis 2a3. Even so, the indirect effect of early child risk mediated by early parenting risk was significant, $\alpha\beta = .02$, $SE = .02$, est./$SE = 0.99$, $p < .05$, indicating an indirect effect of child risk on adolescent substance use as mediated by early parenting problems, as hypothesized by 2a4. Controlling for early child risk, the timing of substance-use onset was significantly incremented by early parenting risk, $b = .14$, $SE = .03$, est./$SE = 4.12$, $p < .01$, indicating support for the first part of Hypothesis 2a5. When early parenting risk was included in the model, early child factors, $F(5, 466) < 1$, did not significantly predict adolescent substance use.

In the model with sociocultural factors as the exogenous variable, the relation between the early parenting risk composite and substance-use onset (second part of Hypothesis 2a1) is described above. The relation between the sociocultural risk composite and substance-use onset (second part of Hypothesis 2a2) was tested in the previous chapter. The relation between the sociocultural risk composite and the early parenting risk composite was significant, $b = .49$, $SE = .06$, est./$SE = 7.95$, $p < .01$, supporting the second part of Hypothesis 2a3. The indirect effect of early sociocultural risk mediated by early parenting risk was significant, $\alpha\beta = .05$, $SE = .02$, est./$SE = 2.42$, $p < .05$, supporting the second part of Hypothesis 2a4 and indicating that early parenting problems significantly mediated the effect of sociocultural disadvantage on adolescent substance use. Finally, even when controlling for sociocultural risk, timing of substance-use onset was significantly incremented by early parenting risk, $b = .10$, $SE = .04$, est./$SE = 2.54$, $p < .05$, supporting the second part of Hypothesis 2a5. When early parenting risk was included in the model, however, sociocultural factors did not significantly predict substance use, $F(7, 994) = 1.72$, ns.

Early Parenting as a Mediator of the Relation Between Child/Sociocultural Factors and Early Conduct Problems

Next, early parenting problems were tested as a predictor and mediator of the effects of early child factors and sociocultural factors on early conduct problems, in separate models. For the model with early child factors, early parenting risk significantly predicted early conduct problems, $b = .15$, $SE = .04$, est./$SE = 3.97$, $p < .01$, supporting Hypothesis 2b1. Early conduct problems were not significantly predicted by early child risk factors, $r = .08$, ns, a finding that is not consistent with Hypothesis 2b2. The test of Hypothesis 2b3 was reported above. Early parenting risk also significantly mediated the effect of early child risk on conduct problems, $\alpha\beta = .02$, $SE = .02$, est./$SE = 1.00$, $p < .05$, consistent with Hypothesis 2b4. Even when child risk factors were controlled, early parenting risk significantly incremented the prediction of conduct problems, $b = .18$, $SE = .03$, est./$SE = 5.41$, $p < .01$, consistent with Hypothesis 2b5. When early parenting risk was included in the model, child factors did not significantly predict early conduct problems, $t(152) < 1$, ns.

In the model testing sociocultural risk, as reported already, early parenting risk significantly predicted early conduct problems (second part of Hypothesis 2b1). The sociocultural risk composite significantly predicted conduct problems, $r = .22$, $p < .001$, supporting the second part of Hypothesis 2b2. The relation between the sociocultural risk composite and the early parenting risk composite was significant, $b = .49$, $SE = .06$, est./$SE = 7.70$, $p < .01$, supporting Hypothesis 2b3. The indirect effect of early sociocultural risk mediated by early parenting risk was significant, $\alpha\beta = .07$, $SE = .02$, est./$SE = 3.53$, $p < .05$, indicating support for Hypothesis 2b4 that early parenting problems would significantly mediate the effect of sociocultural disadvantage on early behavior problems. Even when sociocultural risk factors were controlled, early parenting risk significantly incremented the prediction of conduct problems, $b = .15$, $SE = .04$, est./$SE = 3.95$, $p < .01$, consistent with Hypothesis 2b5. When early parenting risk was included in the model, sociocultural risk factors did not significantly predict early conduct problems, $b = .10$, $SE = .05$, $t(152) = 1.76$, ns.

DISCUSSION

Several novel sets of findings from this chapter on early parenting effects make important contributions to the field. The first set concerns the role of early parenting dysfunction in substance-use onset. It was found that early parenting factors (especially nonmaternal child care, lack of father involvement, high interparental conflict, and parents' support for the use of aggression in problem solving before the age of 5) significantly predict risk of adolescent substance use, even when early child and sociocultural risk factors are controlled. Parents' interactions with their child at the time of transition to elementary school apparently set into motion a developmental trajectory that leads to adolescent use of substances or protection from that use (Patterson et al., 1991).

Furthermore, parenting practices at the time of school transition partially mediate the effect of early sociocultural risk factors on adolescent substance use and help us understand how sociocultural factors operate. McLoyd (1990) had hypothesized that family poverty exerts its effects on child development through its more direct impact on making parenting difficult. Her hypothesis has been supported in this chapter, through findings that high sociocultural risk (including low SES, single parenthood, and teen pregnancy) is associated with less involved parenting and more aggressive modeling, and the mediational analysis that these parenting practices statistically account for part of the effect of high sociocultural risk on youth outcomes in substance use.

Not only does early parenting dysfunction provide the process through which sociocultural risk exerts its impact, it provides incremental risk beyond that imposed by earlier factors. The cascade toward substance use is enhanced by early parenting dysfunction.

The findings also point toward a path that could explain how early parenting dysfunction might exert a long-term effect on adolescent substance use. It was found that early parenting variables predicted early child conduct problems and mediated the impact of sociocultural factors on the development of child conduct problems. These findings are consistent with those reported by Dodge et al. (1994a) and with independent findings by Sampson and Laub (1994) with the sample from the Glueck study of delinquency.

VI. EARLY CHILD BEHAVIOR PROBLEM FACTORS

Following the cascade model, the next question to be addressed in this study concerned further analyses of the mechanisms through which early parenting risk factors might lead to adolescent substance use. It was found in the previous chapter that early parenting dysfunction predicts child conduct problems. After reviewing the literature, Glantz and Leshner (2000) argued that child conduct problems are the single strongest predictor of adolescent substance use. It was hypothesized that the child's conduct problems would predict later substance-use onset and would mediate the development of adolescent substance-use problems.

Several literatures suggest how conduct problems might play a role in the dynamic cascade toward substance use. The first literature concerns the antecedents of conduct problems. Patterson's (Reid, Patterson, & Snyder, 2000) coercive social learning theory asserts a process between parent and child that leads the child to learn coercive behavioral habits that transfer to the external world. According to this functionalist perspective, children who begin to display antisocial behaviors such as aggression and disruptiveness in the early school years have been inadvertently trained in the effectiveness of these behaviors by parents. Snyder, Reid, and Patterson (2003) describe coercion training as a four-step process that starts with aversive intrusions by a family member into the child's activities, which are met by the child with counterattacks that lead the parent to stop any demands for compliance (called negative reinforcement), which the child reinforces by stopping the counterattack. The coercion training process is a reciprocal family dynamic that leads the child to learn to use antisocial tactics for instrumental gain.

Gershoff's (2002) meta-analysis has revealed a consistent association between corporal punishment and child aggressive behavior, although the interpretation of that association is still in doubt (Benjet & Kazdin, 2003). Longitudinal investigations support the relation between early parental punishment and later antisocial behavior. McCord's (1991) analyses of the Cambridge–Somerville Youth Study indicate that fathers' use of physical punishment predicts sons' adult criminal records, even when paternal criminality was controlled. Farrington and Hawkins (1991) found that harsh discipline practices at age 8 predict later delinquency in their sample of 411 London males from the Cambridge Longitudinal Study. Other parenting factors also predict child conduct problems, including lack of parental warmth and exposure to nonparental child care (Dodge, Coie, & Lynam, 2006). Thus, it was hypothesized that early parenting dysfunction would predict the child's development of chronic aggressive behaviors toward peers during elementary school.

The second relevant literature concerns the link between parental socialization of a child and the child's peer relations as mediated by the child's behavioral conduct. Parents' influences on their child's peer relationships have been identified by social development scholars for some time (e.g., Grimes, Klein, & Putallaz, 2004; Kerns, 1998). Putallaz, Klein, Costanzo, and Hedges (1994) found that parents' conceptions of their own peer relationships and their framing of their goals for their child influenced their child's behavioral competence during group entry interactions with peers. Grimes et al. (2004) reported that the warmth of parents' relationships with their child influences the child's peer relationships. Prinstein and LaGreca (1999) found that parents' own social competence and concepts about peer relations predicted their child's social competence with peers. Thus, the quality of the parents' relationship with their child and their conceptions about parenting and peer relationships are hypothesized to exert influence on the child's antisocial behavior patterns and success in peer relationships.

The following hypotheses thus address the role of early child conduct problems in predicting, mediating, and incrementing adolescent substance use, as well as in predicting early peer relations:

H3a1: The set of conduct problems factors will predict adolescent substance use.

H3a2: The set of early dysfunctional parenting factors will predict adolescent substance use (already supported in previous chapter).

H3a3: The set of early dysfunctional parenting factors will predict conduct problems.

H3a4: The set of conduct problems factors will partially mediate the effect of dysfunctional parenting factors on adolescent substance use.

H3a5: The set of conduct problems factors will increment the prediction of adolescent substance use beyond the level predicted by dysfunctional parenting factors.

H3b1: The set of conduct problems variables will predict early peer relations problems.

H3b2: The set of dysfunctional parenting variables will predict early peer relations problems.

H3b3: The set of dysfunctional parenting variables will predict early conduct problems (as in Hypothesis 3a3).

H3b4: The set of early conduct problems factors will partially mediate the effect of dysfunctional parenting factors on early peer relations problems.

H3b5: The set of early conduct problems factors will increment the prediction of early peer relations problems beyond the level predicted by dysfunctional parenting factors.

RESULTS

Prediction of Adolescent Substance Use From Early Conduct Problems

The conduct problems risk factors, taken together, significantly predicted substance-use onset, $F(2, 1524) = 7.39$, $p < .001$, supporting Hypothesis 3a1 (see Table 9 for parameter estimates). Each of the two predictors in this cluster was tested independently in relation to the onset of illicit substance use. The externalizing behavior problems score significantly predicted substance-use onset, $HR = 1.28$, 95% CI: 1.11, 1.47, $t(566) = 3.40$, $p < .001$; internalizing behavior did not, $HR = 0.95$, 95% CI: 0.83, 1.08, $t(1310) < 1$, ns. None of the tests for interactions with the time of measurement showed statistical significance, $ps > .05$.

In the model with both predictor variables, externalizing behavior problems uniquely predicted an increase in hazard, $HR = 1.31$, 95% CI: 1.14, 1.51, $t(653) = 3.71$, $p < .001$. High internalizing behavior problems were marginally associated with a reduction in hazard, $HR = 0.89$, 95% CI: 0.77, 1.02, $t(1616) = 1.65$, $p < .10$.

TABLE 9

SUBSTANCE-USE ONSET PREDICTION FROM EACH EARLY CHILD BEHAVIOR PROBLEM FACTOR

Predictor	Hazard Ratio (95% CI)	t	df	p
Internalizing behavior problems	0.95 (0.83, 1.08)	<1	1310	ns
Externalizing behavior problems	1.28 (1.11, 1.47)	3.40	566	<.001

Note. $N = 585$. Tabled values are hazard ratios per standard deviation change in predictor.

Early Conduct Problems as a Mediator of the Relation Between Early Parenting and Substance Use

The mediational model hypothesized that early conduct problems would mediate the effect of early parenting problems on substance use. As noted earlier, early parenting dysfunction significantly predicted adolescent substance use (Hypothesis 3a2). The prediction of conduct problems from the early parenting problems composite was significant, $b = .19$, $SE = .03$, est./$SE = 5.67$, $p < .01$, supporting Hypothesis 3a3. Next, the indirect effect of early parenting problems mediated by early conduct problems was significant, $\alpha\beta = .03$, $SE = .01$, est./$SE = 2.44$, $p < .05$, indicating support for Hypothesis 3a4 that early conduct problems would mediate the effect of early parenting problems on substance use. Even controlling for early parenting problems, early behavior problems significantly incremented the prediction of substance use, $b = .44$, $SE = .06$, est./$SE = 7.02$, $p < .01$, supporting Hypothesis 3a5. Finally, when the early behavior problems variable was included in the model, early parenting problems still significantly incremented substance use, $b = .12$, $SE = .04$, est./$SE = 3.16$, $p < .01$, indicating that the mediation was only partial.

Early Conduct Problems as a Mediator of the Relation Between Early Parenting and Early Peer Relations Problems

Early conduct problems were tested as a mediator of the effects of early parenting problems on early peer relations problems. As reported in previous analyses, early conduct problems significantly predicted early peer relations problems, supporting Hypothesis 3b1. Early parenting dysfunction significantly predicted early peer relations problems, $r = .23$, $p < .001$, supporting Hypothesis 3b2. The prediction of early conduct problems from the early parenting problems composite was also significant, $b = .19$, $SE = .03$, est./$SE = 5.67$, $p < .01$, supporting Hypothesis 3b3. The indirect effect of early parenting problems as mediated by early behavior problems was significant, $\alpha\beta = .08$, $SE = .02$, est./$SE = 4.41$, $p < .05$, indicating support for Hypothesis 3b4 that early behavior problems mediate the effect of early parenting problems on early peer relations problems.

Early peer relations problems were also significantly predicted from early behavior problems, $b = .44$, $SE = .06$, est./$SE = 7.02$, $p < .01$, even controlling for early parenting problems, supporting Hypothesis 3b5. Finally, even when early conduct problems were included in the model, the direct effect of early parenting problems on early peer relations problems was significant, $b = .16$, $SE = .05$, est./$SE = 3.43$, $p < .01$, indicating that mediation was only partial.

DISCUSSION

The findings join a long list of studies demonstrating the role of early externalizing conduct problems in the developmental pathway toward substance-use onset in adolescence (Glantz & Leshner, 2000). In contrast, when the correlation with externalizing problems was controlled, early internalizing problems did not significantly predict adolescent substance use, also consistent with past findings (Kaplow et al., 2001).

A novel contribution of these findings concerns the role of early externalizing conduct problems as a mediator of the impact of early parenting on substance-use outcomes. Conduct problems were predicted from prior parenting problems (as previously found by numerous investigators, Dodge, Coie, & Lynam, 2006) and mediated the impact of early parenting problems on substance-use outcomes. These findings shed light on the mechanisms through which early parenting exerts its impact and strengthen the case for externalizing behavior problems as a critical factor in the developmental cascade toward substance use.

The findings also indicate how conduct problems might operate in leading to substance use. It was found that early conduct problems predict subsequent problems in peer relations and mediate the impact of early dysfunctional parenting on peer relations difficulties. The cascade toward substance use begins with early structural sociocultural risk factors, which lead to early parenting dysfunction, which leads to child conduct problems, which lead to problems in early peer relations.

Finally, one null finding may be important for the field: Internalizing problems during elementary school were found *not* to predict early-onset substance use, controlling for early externalizing problems. Apparently, youth do not tend to drift toward early substance use out of internalizing problems of anxiety and depression. It remains plausible that self-medication to relieve anxiety or depression is a functional role of substance use in later adolescence or adulthood, but it appears that early-onset substance use is more directly tied to externalizing problems and problems with peers.

VII. EARLY PEER RELATIONS PROBLEM FACTORS

Although early childhood conduct problems are a robust empirical predictor of adolescent substance use, the mechanisms of this effect are not yet clear. We assert here that one major process involves the impact of conduct problems on a child's peer relations (Dodge, Coie, & Lynam, 2006). An abundance of literature supports the hypothesis that externalizing behavior problems lead peers to reject a child and to isolate him or her from the mainstream peer group (Rubin, Bukowski, & Laursen, 2008).

In turn, a large body of research supports the hypothesis that lack of success in peer relationships in elementary school, as indexed by low social preference among peers, is a strong marker of a variety of adolescent deviant outcomes, including substance use (Kupersmidt, Coie, & Dodge, 1990). The added conflict and stress that peer rejection brings, along with lost opportunities to learn social skills through interaction with competent peers, exacerbates conduct problems (Dodge et al., 2003) and may pose a risk for adolescent substance use as well as mediate the impact of conduct problems on substance use. Thus, it was hypothesized that measures of peer relationship success in elementary school would predict adolescent substance use and would mediate the effect of previous conduct problems on substance-use outcomes.

It was further hypothesized that a more proximal effect of problems in childhood peer relations would be to exacerbate problems in parenting during early adolescence. Peer relations problems bring stress for parents, who must respond to complaints by the school, community, and parents of other children. It was hypothesized that parents would cope with this stress by withdrawing their supervision and monitoring of children during adolescence as a way to reduce overt stress.

The following hypotheses assert the role of early peer relations problems in predicting, mediating, and incrementing adolescent substance use and subsequent adolescent parenting problems.

H4a1: The set of early peer relations problems factors will predict adolescent substance use.

H4a2: The set of early conduct problems factors will predict adolescent substance use (already previously demonstrated).

H4a3: The set of early conduct problems factors will predict early peer relations problems.

H4a4: The set of early peer relations factors will partially mediate the effect of early conduct problems factors on adolescent substance use.

H4a5: The set of early peer relations factors will increment the prediction of adolescent substance use beyond the level predicted by child conduct problems factors.

H4b1: The set of early peer relations problems factors will predict adolescent parenting problems.

H4b2: The set of early conduct problems factors will predict adolescent parenting problems.

H4b3: The set of early conduct problems factors will predict early peer relations problems (as in Hypothesis 4a3).

H4b4: The set of early peer relations problems will partially mediate the effect of early conduct problems on adolescent parenting problems.

H4b5: The set of early peer relations factors will increment the prediction of adolescent substance use beyond the level predicted by early conduct problems factors.

RESULTS

Prediction of Substance Use From Early Peer Relations Problems

The early peer relations risk factors, taken as a set, significantly predicted substance use, $F(3, 2276) = 2.96$, $p < .05$, supporting Hypothesis 4a1. Each of the three predictors in this cluster was tested independently in relation to the onset of illicit substance use. Low social preference scores and peer rejection significantly predicted substance-use onset; parameter estimates and test statistics are presented in Table 10. None of the tests for interactions with the time of measurement showed statistical significance, all $ps > .05$.

TABLE 10

SUBSTANCE-USE ONSET PREDICTION FROM EACH EARLY PEER RELATIONS FACTOR

Predictor	Hazard Ratio (95% CI)	t	df	p
Social preference	0.82 (0.72, 0.94)	2.93	1991	.003
Peer rejection[a]	1.61 (1.05, 2.45)	2.19	444	.029
Years rejected[a]	1.12 (0.94, 1.33)	1.29	781	ns

Note. $N = 585$. Tabled values are hazard ratios per standard deviation change in predictor, or unit change for categorical variables (marked).
[a]Categorical.

In the full model, social preference showed a significant unique effect. High social preference scores were associated with a reduction in hazard, $HR = 0.84$, 95% CI: 0.70, 1.00, $t(1818) = 1.98$, ns.

Early Peer Relations Problems as a Mediator of the Relation Between Early Behavior Problems and Substance Use

The mediational model at this step hypothesized that early peer relations problems would mediate the effect of early behavior problems on substance use. As reported earlier, early conduct problems significantly predicted adolescent substance use (Hypothesis 4a2). The prediction of peer relations problems from the early conduct problems composite was significant, $b = .50$, $SE = .06$, est./$SE = 9.18$, $p < .01$, supporting Hypothesis 4a3. The early peer relations problems composite significantly mediated the impact of early conduct problems on substance use, $\alpha\beta = .02$, $SE = .02$, est./$SE = 1.35$, $p < .05$, indicating support for Hypothesis 4a4 that early peer relations problems would mediate the effect of early behavior problems on substance use. Also, substance-use onset was significantly predicted from early peer relations problems, even with early conduct problems in the model, $b = .17$, $SE = .06$, est./$SE = 2.95$, $p < .01$, consistent with Hypothesis 4a5. When early peer relations problems were included in the model, early conduct problems did not significantly predict substance use, $b = .05$, $SE = .04$, est./$SE = 1.36$, ns.

Early Peer Relations Problems as a Mediator of the Relation Between Early Conduct Problems and Adolescent Parenting

The prediction of adolescent parenting problems from the early peer relations composite was significant, $b = .11$, $SE = .04$, est./$SE = 2.87$, $p < .01$, supporting Hypothesis 4b1. Adolescent parenting problems was significantly predicted from early conduct problems, $r = .14$, $p < .05$, supporting Hypothesis 4b2, and early peer relations was significantly predicted from early conduct problems, supporting Hypothesis 4b3. Early peer relations

68

problems was found to mediate the effect of early conduct problems on adolescent parenting problems, $\alpha\beta = .06$, $SE = .02$, est./$SE = 2.71$, $p < .05$, supporting Hypothesis 4b4. Early peer relations problems also significantly incremented the prediction of adolescent parenting problems beyond early conduct problems, $b = .11$, $SE = .04$, est./$SE = 2.89$, $p < .01$, consistent with Hypothesis 4b5. When early peer relations problems were included in the model, adolescent parenting problems were not significantly predicted from early conduct problems, $b = .10$, $SE = .06$, est./$SE = 1.74$, ns.

DISCUSSION

Several findings are most important from these analyses. First, peer relationships problems in elementary school were found to predict adolescent substance use and to be incremental predictors of use. Second, these problems were found to mediate the impact of early parenting factors on adolescent substance use. Third, peer relationship problems were found to mediate a crucial shift in parenting practices, from early unavailability of parents and exposure to aggressive models to later withdrawal from supervision and monitoring.

Problems in relating to peers, as indexed by low social preference, status as rejected in the classroom peer group, and disruptive behavior toward peers, have been related to a broad array of later maladjustment outcomes (cf. Kupersmidt et al., 1990), but the current study adds to the literature by indicating the risk for early-onset substance use during middle school. This alarming finding should increase the focus on improving peer relations as a broad preventive intervention.

The other findings enhance understanding of the processes through which early peer relations problems might operate on the development of substance use, by identifying the antecedents and consequences of peer relations problems. Parents who are less involved in their children's lives, who have more interparental conflict, and who support the use of aggression in problem solving have children who come to have difficulties in relating effectively with peers, which then propels a cascade of problems over time, including adolescent substance use. The role of parents in promoting skills in peer relations has been proposed by Grimes et al. (2004) and Prinstein and LaGreca (1999), and these findings support that assertion.

The third finding is novel to the field in describing the transactional nature of the relation between parenting and peer relations. It was found that early nonmaternal child care, lack of paternal involvement, interparental conflict, and parental support for aggression in problem solving transform into withdrawal from monitoring and supervision of a child, partially through the mediating mechanism of the child's growth of peer problems. That is, a 5-year-old child who experiences extensive nonmaternal child care, lack of paternal involvement, interparental conflict, and parental support for aggression in problem solving is likely to develop problems with peers. In turn, high rates of peer problems (which probably lead to numerous teacher reports to parents of child problems) are met, ironically, by *less* monitoring and supervision by parents over time. The pattern is ironic and unfortunate because it is the children who display problems with peers who *most* need parental monitoring and supervision during early adolescence. This finding brings a crucial insight into children's social development: Parenting practices evolve over time, partially in response to children's behavior, and cascade into higher levels of problematic patterns through a dynamic transaction among parent, child, and the peer group.

VIII. ADOLESCENT PARENTING FACTORS

The next set of questions addressed the role of parenting during early adolescence in the development of adolescent substance use. A large literature implicates parents' lack of adequate monitoring and supervision in correlating with, and predicting, adolescents' substance use (Fletcher, Steinberg, & Wheeler-Williams, 2004) and a broad array of other deviant behaviors (Dodge, Coie, & Lynam, 2006). This step is hypothesized as a crucial catalyst of adolescents' movement toward substance use.

The cascade model posits not only that parenting factors in early adolescence will predict substance use but also that they will mediate the impact of earlier problems in peer relations on substance use. The earlier problems with peers are hypothesized to lead to increased conflict between the parent and youth. Instead of continuing to attempt to discipline the youth through strategies of harsh punishment, the parent begins to withdraw from the relationship with the youth. In a sense, the early adolescent period may mark the beginning of the parent's giving up on the child. Withdrawal from conflict may bring immediate relief from stress for the parent, but withdrawal from the parental roles of supervision, monitoring, and application of consequences for misbehavior propels the youth toward substance use.

In turn, the cascade model posits that failures in parental supervision operate on adolescent substance use by opening the youth's door to the deviant peer group. That is, it was hypothesized that a major proximal outcome of parents' lack of supervision is that the youth becomes free to drift toward exposure to new deviant influences, which bring sensation value, models for behavior, exposure to substances, and reinforcement of deviant behavior through a process called deviancy training (Dishion & Owen, 2002).

Thus, the following set of hypotheses asserts the role of parenting problems during early adolescence in predicting, mediating, and incrementing substance use and adolescent peer relations problems.

H5a1: The set of early adolescent parenting factors will predict adolescent substance use.

H5a2: The set of early peer relations factors will predict adolescent substance use (already reported, above).

H5a3: The set of early peer relations factors will predict early adolescent parenting factors.

H5a4: The set of adolescent parenting factors will partially mediate the effect of early peer relations factors on adolescent substance use.

H5a5: The set of adolescent parenting factors will increment the prediction of adolescent substance use beyond the level predicted by early peer relations factors.

H5b1: The set of adolescent parenting factors will predict adolescent peer relations problems.

H5b2: The set of early peer relations problems will predict adolescent peer relations problems.

H5b3: The set of early peer relations problems will predict adolescent parenting problems (as in Hypothesis 5a3).

H5b4: The set of adolescent parenting problems will partially mediate the effect of early peer relations problems on adolescent peer relations problems.

H5b5: The set of adolescent parenting factors will increment the prediction of adolescent peer relations problems beyond the level predicted by early peer relations problems.

RESULTS

Prediction of Substance Use From Adolescent Parenting

The two adolescent parenting risk factors, taken together, significantly predicted onset of substance use, $F(2, 453) = 10.54$, $p < .001$, supporting Hypothesis 5a1 (parameter estimates are listed in Table 11). Each predictor in this pair was tested independently in relation to the onset of illicit substance use; both were significantly related to substance use. Parent report of parental supervision predicted reduced hazard of substance-use onset,

TABLE 11

Predictor	Hazard Ratio (95% CI)	t	df	p
Parental supervision (mother report)	− .21 (− .39, − .02)	2.20	245	.029
Parental supervision (adolescent report)	− .20 (− .38, − .03)	2.26	206	.025

Note. $N = 585$. Tabled values are hazard ratios per standard deviation change in predictor.

$HR = 0.76$, 95% CI $= 0.66$, 0.87, $t(455) = 3.94$, $p < .001$, as did adolescent report of parental supervision, $HR = 0.76$, 95% CI $= 0.65$, 0.90, $t(193) = 3.35$, $p < .001$. Interactions with timing of onset were not significant, $ps > .05$. In the model with both variables, both parent and youth reports of parental supervision continued to show significant unique prediction, mother report: $HR = 0.79$, 95% CI $= 0.68$, 0.92, $t(332) = 3.06$, $p < .01$, adolescent report: $HR = 0.81$, 95% CI $= 0.68$, 0.95, $t(183) = 2.61$, $p < .01$.

Adolescent Parenting as a Mediator of the Relation Between Early Peer Relations and Substance Use

The association between early peer relations and adolescent substance use was reported previously to be significant (Hypothesis 5a2). The relation between early peer relations problems and adolescent parenting problems was significant, $b = .13$, $SE = .04$, est./$SE = 3.62$, $p < .01$, supporting Hypothesis 5a3. The indirect effect of early peer relations problems as mediated by adolescent parenting problems was significant, $\alpha\beta = .03$, $SE = .01$, est./$SE = 2.95$, $p < .05$, indicating support for Hypothesis 5a4 that adolescent parenting problems would mediate the effect of early peer relations problems on substance use. Substance-use onset was significantly predicted by adolescent parenting problems, $b = .22$, $SE = .04$, est./$SE = 5.10$, $p < .01$, even when early peer relations problems were included in the model, supporting Hypothesis 5a5. When adolescent parenting problems were included in the model, early peer relations problems no longer significantly predicted substance use, $b = .06$, $SE = .03$, est./$SE = 1.65$, *ns*.

Adolescent Parenting as a Mediator of the Relation Between Early Peer Relations and Adolescent Peer Relations

As noted previously, adolescent parenting problems significantly predicted subsequent problems in adolescent peer relations, supporting Hypothesis 5b1. Early peer relations significantly predicted adolescent peer relations, $b = .15$, $SE = .05$, est./$SE = 2.85$, $p < .01$, supporting Hypothesis 5b2. As reported previously, the relation between early peer relations problems and adolescent parenting problems was significant, supporting

Hypothesis 5b3. The indirect effect of early peer relations problems as mediated by adolescent parenting problems was significant, $\alpha\beta = .08$, $SE = .02$, est./$SE = 3.34$, $p < .05$, indicating support for Hypothesis 5b4 that adolescent parenting problems mediate the effect of early peer relations problems on later peer relations problems. Even when early peer relations problems were included in the model, adolescent parenting problems significantly incremented the prediction of adolescent peer relations problems, $b = .60$, $SE = .07$, est./$SE = 8.59$, $p < .01$, supporting Hypothesis 5b5. Finally, when adolescent parenting problems were included, early peer relations problems did not show a significant direct effect on adolescent peer problems, $b = .07$, $SE = .05$, est./$SE = 1.43$, ns.

DISCUSSION

The findings presented here offer support for the role of parenting practices in early adolescence as a crucial step in the development of adolescent substance use and provide insight into the processes through this effect might occur. The finding that parental lack of monitoring and supervision predict adolescent substance use is consistent with the field's general conclusions (cf. Fletcher, Steinberg, & Wheeler-Williams, 2004), but the current finding adds to that literature by controlling for previous child behavior and peer relations problems, thus increasing one's confidence that parenting practices have an impact rather than being merely epiphenomenal to the process.

Furthermore, the findings offer an understanding of the processes through which early adolescent parenting behaviors develop and operate to have an impact on the youth. Findings indicate that parental lack of supervision is a mechanism through which early child peer relations difficulties grow into adolescent substance use: Parents respond to early child peer difficulties by withdrawing their monitoring and supervision, which opens the door for the child to engage in substance use unfettered by parental constraints.

The findings also describe the process through which parental supervision problems may lead to adolescent substance use. That is, inadequate supervision by parents was found to predict the youth's association with deviant peers as friends and the deviant peer group as a primary peer context. The role of the deviant peer group in substance-use onset was examined in the next set of analyses.

IX. ADOLESCENT PEER CONTEXT FACTORS

Association with deviant peers has long been posited as one of the most robust predictors of deviant adolescent behavior in a broad array of domains, including substance use (Gifford-Smith, Dodge, Dishion, & McCord, 2005). This dimension of peer relations in adolescence is orthogonal to contemporaneous peer social acceptance/rejection; in fact, the association between peer popularity and membership in a deviant peer network shifts from slightly negative to slightly positive during the early adolescent years (Cillessen & Mayeux, 2004). Association with deviant peers is predictable from earlier social rejection; however, findings that are consistent with a developmental trend for early peer-rejected children to gravitate toward a deviant peer group in an effort to gain social acceptance.

The processes through which deviant peer associations influence the onset of substance use are many, as described by Dishion in a theory of deviancy training (Dishion & Owen, 2002; Dishion, Capaldi, Spracklen, & Li, 1995). Along with neighborhood factors of lack of safety and exposure to drug trade, they provide a context in which substance use can be initiated.

A critical question in the relation between deviant peer association and deviant behavior has been the direction of effect. Selection factors (called homophily here) do operate (Kandel, 1978), but carefully analyzed longitudinal data reveal that associating with a deviant peer group escalates engagement in deviant behavior, and withdrawal from association with deviant peers is followed by reductions in deviant behavior (Thornberry et al., 1993). The mechanisms of this effect are probably numerous, including positive reinforcement of deviant behavior, increased opportunities for deviance, and deviancy training (Dishion & Dodge, 2006).

A major methodological problem of research in this domain has been the predominant reliance on youth self-report for assessment of both the deviant peer group and one's own behavior (Bagwell et al., 2000). Reporter biases and the possibility that it is a youth's perception of peer activity rather than the peers' actual behavior that drives this association render the exclusive use of self-report as a problem. In the current study, youth, teachers', and parents' reports provided a multirater assessment of deviant peer associations.

The current study tested the hypotheses that association with a deviant peer group during the middle school years would be associated with early-onset substance use and that deviant peer associations would mediate the effect of poor parental supervision on substance use. These hypotheses are premised on the supposition that high parental supervision keeps youth from gravitating toward deviant peers. Although many youth would not move in this direction even without close parental supervision, children who have been rejected by peers in elementary school might be at high risk for this movement. These hypotheses assert the role of adolescent peer relations problems in predicting, mediating, and incrementing substance use:

H6a1: Adverse adolescent peer relations will predict subsequent substance-use onset.

H6a2: Problems in parenting during early adolescence will predict subsequent substance use (as found earlier).

H6a3: Problems in parenting during early adolescence will predict problems in adolescent peer relations.

H6a4: Adverse adolescent peer relations will mediate the effect of adolescent parenting problems on substance use.

H6a5: Adverse adolescent peer context will increment the prediction of adolescent substance use beyond the level predicted by adolescent parenting problems.

RESULTS

Prediction of Substance Use From Adolescent Peer Relations Problems

The eight adolescent peer relations variables, taken as a set, significantly predicted onset of substance use, $F(8, 2{,}767) = 9.27$, $p < .001$, supporting Hypothesis 6a1. Each of the eight variables in the adolescent context cluster was tested independently as a predictor of onset of substance use. Six variables (including Grade-6 self-reported peer drug use; Grade-7 self-reported peer-group deviance, peer-group drug use, best-friend deviance, and susceptibility to peer pressure; and Grade-7 teacher-reported peer deviance) were significantly related to a youth's own later substance-use onset, $p < .05$, as shown in Table 12.

76

TABLE 12

SUBSTANCE-USE ONSET PREDICTION FROM EACH ADOLESCENT PEER RELATIONS RISK FACTOR

Predictor	Hazard Ratio (95% CI)	t	df	p
Grade 7 neighborhood safety	0.96 (0.84, 1.10)	<1	1327	ns
Grade 6 peer drug use (mother report)	1.05 (0.92, 1.21)	<1	517	ns
Early	1.30 (1.02, 1.67)	2.10	2750	.036
Late	0.99 (0.83, 1.17)	<1	346	ns
Grade 6 peer drug use (self-report)	1.20 (1.05, 1.37)	2.68	743	.007
Grade 7 peer group deviance (self-report)	1.15 (0.95, 1.40)	1.41	443	ns
Early	2.38 (1.62, 3.49)	4.45	760	<.001
Late	1.42 (1.22, 1.65)	4.51	556	<.001
Grade 7 peer group drug use (self-report)	1.37 (1.20, 1.58)	4.51	380	<.001
Early	1.81 (1.40, 2.33)	4.57	2506	<.001
Late	1.26 (1.06, 1.49)	2.69	243	<.008
Grade 7 best friend deviance (self-report)	1.46 (1.27, 1.68)	5.30	552	<.001
Early	2.46 (1.66, 3.66)	4.47	406	<.001
Late	1.34 (1.15, 1.57)	3.73	422	<.001
Grade 7 susceptibility to peer pressure	1.76 (1.51, 2.04)	7.26	573	<.001
Early	2.75 (1.80, 4.18)	4.72	547	<.001
Late	1.63 (1.38, 1.93)	5.71	429	<.001
Grade 7 peer deviance (teacher report)	1.26 (1.08, 1.48)	2.92	186	<.004
Early	1.85 (1.31, 2.61)	3.53	684	<.001
Late	1.18 (0.99, 1.40)	1.90	192	<.059

Note. N = 585. Tabled values are hazard ratios per standard deviation change in predictor.

Six variables (including grade 6 mother-reported peer drug use; Grade 7 self-reported peer group deviance, peer group drug use, best friend deviance, and susceptibility to peer pressure; and Grade 7 teacher-reported peer deviance) revealed marginal or significant interactions with the time of substance-use measurement; test statistics appear in Table 13. In all cases, the specific relation to early onset of substance use by Grade 7 was stronger than the relation for later onset after that point. For most cases, both pa-

TABLE 13

INTERACTIONS WITH TIMING OF SUBSTANCE-USE ONSET

Predictor	t	df	p
Peer drug use (mother report)	1.83	1298	.068
Peer group deviance	2.42	539	.016
Peer group drug use	2.28	600	.023
Best friend deviance	2.73	312	.007
Susceptibility to peer pressure	2.20	373	.028
Peer deviance (teacher report)	2.31	512	.021

Note. N = 585.

rameter estimates were significantly different from zero, indicating that the effect of adolescent peer context on substance remained significant across time; only the magnitude of effect varied.

In the model with all variables, adolescent-reported peer drug use, $HR = 1.20$, 95% CI: 1.05, 1.37, $t(743) = 2.68$, $p = .007$, and susceptibility to peer pressure, $HR = 1.52$, 95% CI: 1.28, 1.81, $t(448) = 4.76$, $p < .001$, provided significant unique increments in predicting one's own substance use.

Adolescent Peer Relations as a Mediator of the Relation Between Adolescent Parenting Problems and Substance Use

Dysfunctional adolescent parenting significantly predicted an adolescent's substance-use onset (Hypothesis 6a2, as reported earlier), as well as entry into deviant peer associations, $b = .62$, $SE = .07$, est./$SE = 8.96$, $p < .01$, supporting Hypothesis 6a3. The indirect effect of adolescent parenting problems on substance use as mediated by adolescent deviant peer associations was significant, $\alpha\beta = .18$, $SE = .03$, est./$SE = 6.77$, $p < .05$, indicating support for Hypothesis 6a4. A deviant adolescent peer context significantly incremented the prediction of substance-use onset even when adolescent parenting problems were included in the model, $b = .29$, $SE = .03$, est./$SE = 10.36$, $p < .01$, supporting Hypothesis 6a5. Finally, adolescent parenting did not show a direct effect on substance-use onset when adolescent peer context was included in the model, $b = .06$, $SE = .05$, est./$SE = 1.33$, ns, indicating that the mediation by adolescent peer relations was full.

DISCUSSION

As hypothesized, association with deviant peers was found to be robustly related to the subsequent onset of substance use. This finding joins a long literature but also extends it by controlling for previous parental supervision problems, which have confounded some past analyses. These findings join the growing literature implicating the deviant peer group as a training ground for the onset and exacerbation of an array of deviant behaviors during adolescence, including illicit drug use.

The findings provide support for the hypothesis that association with deviant peers is also a mechanism through which inadequate parental supervision exerts its impact on substance-use development. These findings provide a novel contribution by supporting the hypothesis that parental supervision exerts its effect on substance use by freeing high-risk youth to associate with deviant peers, leading to their substance use.

78

X. TESTING THE FULL MODEL

The significant bivariate correlations across the domains of variables make up a tangled web, as depicted in Figure 3. However, the findings described in each chapter provide building blocks for a parsimonious comprehensive model of how substance use develops across childhood and adolescence. The next set of data analyses tested the full model. Each set of variables was combined into a composite using partial least-squares (PLS) analyses and then tested as a sequential predictor of the next set of variables. The hypothesis that this sequential model would provide an optimal fit to the data was tested. Several plausible alternate models were also tested, including a model that relaxed assertions about full mediation and a model that asserted that early child variables predicted all downstream variables with no mediation.

The following hypotheses concern the entire set of predictor variables:

H7a: The entire set of composites of predictor variables across all domains will predict adolescent substance use.

H7b: Each set of variables will mediate the effect of all preceding steps in predicting adolescent substance use.

RESULTS

We tested a series of longitudinal models reflecting different theoretical perspectives and statistical assumptions in the progression of the identified constructs through childhood and adolescence. In order to minimize the number of variables being tested, all models used the PLS composite variate for each cluster, predicting an ordinal variable indicating age of onset of substance use. Fit of the various models (based on averages of the fit indices across imputations) is summarized in Table 14.

79

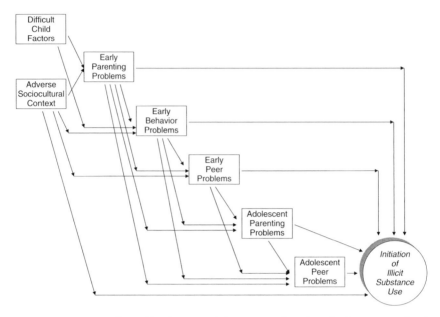

FIGURE 3.—Significant bivariate correlations across domains of substance-use development.

Model 1: The first model was the strictest longitudinal construction. Each variate was allowed to predict only the immediately subsequent variate—that is, all relations to further downstream variables were hypothesized to be fully mediated by the next variate in time. The CFI for this model was only .787, much less than optimal.

Model 2: The second model added two conceptually based paths to Model 1, reflecting paths where full mediation was implausible. Specifically, this model allowed for continuity in parenting and in peer experiences. One

TABLE 14

MODEL FIT STATISTICS FOR LONGITUDINAL MODEL ALTERNATIVES

Model	CFI	TLI	RMSEA
Model 1	.787 (.051)	.729 (.059)	.125 (.016)
Model 2	.917 (.030)	.878 (.047)	.083 (.018)
Model 3	.926 (.033)	.860 (.061)	.088 (.021)
Model 4	.859 (.027)	.704 (.058)	.131 (.016)

Note. N = 585, across 10 imputations. Tabled values are means across imputations, with standard deviations in parentheses.

path was added from Early Parenting to Adolescent Parenting, and one path was added from Early Peer Relations Problems to Adolescent Peer Relations Problems. This model yielded a CFI of .917, which was interpreted as a good fit to the data.

Model 3: The third model relaxed all assumptions of full mediation by single variates. Each variate was regressed on the variate immediately prior and the variate (or variates) immediately before that. This model was included in the testing to provide context for interpreting the fit of Model 2. The CFI was .926, which was negligibly different from the CFI for Model 2. Relaxing the assumption of full mediation did not significantly improve fit.

Model 4: The fourth model reflected an alternate hypothesis, that early child factors would predict adolescent substance use and all other downstream variables, and no other factors would provide an increment to this prediction. The CFI for this model was .859, less than the CFI for Model 2.

Based on these results, we accepted Model 2 as the best compromise between fit and parsimony, although we do note that even the fit of Model 2 could be improved. The Model 2 results are indicated in Table 15. This empirical model is depicted parsimoniously in Figure 4. Model 2 results indicate that child risk and sociocultural context factors accounted for 31% of the variance in early parenting. In turn, early parenting accounted for 12% of the variance in early behavior problems. Early behavior problems accounted 15% of the variance in early peer experiences. Early parenting

TABLE 15

MODEL 2 RESULTS

Outcome (R^2) Predictor	Unstandard Estimate	Standardized Estimate	Standard Error	Est./SE	Two-Tailed p-value
Early parenting (.309)					
Child factors	.102	.077	.077	1.314	ns
Sociocultural context	.536	.544	.058	9.241	<.001
Early behavior problems (.117)					
Early parenting	.232	.342	.035	6.614	<.001
Early peer experiences (.150)					
Early behavior problems	.590	.386	.064	9.235	<.001
Adolescent peer experiences (.139)					
Early peer experiences	.075	.102	.038	2.004	<.05
Early parenting	.261	.343	.036	7.333	<.001
Adolescent peer experiences (.253)					
Adolescent painting	.657	.471	.072	9.114	<.001
Early peer experiences	.119	.116	.051	2.347	<.02
Age of first substance use (.219)					
Adolescent peer experiences	−.316	−.468	.029	−10.953	<.01

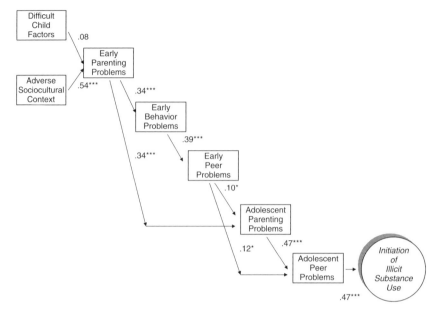

FIGURE 4.—Parsimonious empirical model of substance-use development.

and early peer experiences together accounted for 14% of the variance in adolescent parenting. Early peer experiences and adolescent parenting to-gether accounted for 25% of the variance in adolescent peer experiences. Finally, adolescent peer experiences accounted for 22% of the variance in age of onset of illicit substance use.

DISCUSSION

In full-model testing, the proposed dynamic cascade model received empirical support. The 35 predictor variables could be collated into seven indices. Each index significantly predicted the temporally subsequent in-dex, culminating in the significant prediction of illicit substance use. This model was superior to an alternate model in which full mediation was not required and a model in which a single child risk factor alone accounted for continuity in deviant behavior.

One minor constraint that had not been predicted but in retrospect is obvious is that model fit was improved when the early parenting domain was allowed to predict later parenting, and the early peer domain was allowed to predict the later peer domain. This concession to stability of within-target relationship across time may represent a reality that future environmental experiences do not fully mediate the stability of within-re-lationship processes, or it may be that actual mediating variables went un-measured.

The parsimony of the empirically supported model is striking. An array of correlations across domains can be reduced to a relatively coherent dy-namic cascade across time.

XI. MODERATION BY GENDER

The next analyses addressed the role of gender in substance-use onset. Males are at greater risk than females for both early-onset substance use (Bray, Adams, Getz, & McQueen, 2003; Kaplow et al., 2001) and later-onset substance use (Siebenbruner, Englund, Egeland, & Hudson, 2006). However, recent evidence suggests that female rates are approaching those of males (Johnston et al., 2008). Gender main effects were hypothesized for predictor variables in ways that are consistent with the literature. It was hypothesized that males would display higher levels than females in early conduct problems (Dodge, Coie, & Lynam, 2006), early peer relations problems (Dodge et al., 2003), and adolescent deviant peer associations (Laird et al., 2001).

More important, the generalizability of correlational patterns across gender groups was tested. If developmental processes were found to differ across gender groups, the implications would be huge for basic understanding of both substance-use development and preventive intervention. Modest evidence suggests that developmental processes might operate differently for males and females. Lukas and Wetherington (2005), for example, note that cocaine affects females and males differently when ingested nasally (but not intravenously). Some context factors (such as poverty and peer rejection) exert a similar magnitude and type of effect on boys and girls (Dodge et al., 1994a, 1994b), whereas other factors (e.g., parental contingent response to child misbehavior) affect boys and girls differently (McFadyen-Ketchum et al., 1996).

Although no specific hypotheses were posited, given the scant literature, the need to test for generalizability in developmental processes across groups remains imperative. We employed the logic pioneered by Rowe, Vazsonyi, and Flannery (1994) and tested the hypothesis:

> **H8a:** The most strongly supported empirical model of prediction will differ for males and females.

RESULTS

Table 16 lists means and standard deviations for males and females for all variables. Males were significantly higher than females in father involvement, the experience of harsh discipline, support of aggression, peer social rejection, peer group deviance, best friend deviance, and susceptibility to peer pressure, and lower than females in peer social preference and parental monitoring by mother report. No difference was found between males and females in substance use in any year.

The critical research question was whether gender interacted with any risk variables in predicting substance use. Model 2, described above, was retested, with gender being allowed to moderate all paths. This model did not significantly improve fit beyond the previous "full" model, $\chi^2(8) = 9.71$, *ns*, indicating that within the constraints of empirical model testing, the full model did not prove superior for either males or females. Rather, the model held equally well for both males and females, and the hypothesis of differences was not supported.

TABLE 16

MAIN EFFECTS OF GENDER ON PREDICTOR VARIABLES AND SUBSTANCE-USE ONSET

Predictor	Males ($n = 304$)		Females ($n = 281$)	
	Mean	SD	Mean	SD
Early child risk factors				
Temperamental risk	3.32	0.97	3.27	0.94
Medical complications	1.27	0.53	1.27	0.57
Mother's alcohol use	0.60	1.3	0.61	1.3
Early sociocultural risk factors				
SES	40.37	14.0	38.8	13.9
Single mother	0.204	0.40	0.270	0.44
Adult–child ratio (log)	0.17	0.52	0.21	0.46
Teen pregnancy	0.066	0.25	0.082	0.27
Unplanned pregnancy	2.05	1.14	2.16	1.13
Family stress	7.90	4.37	8.01	4.13
Social isolation	3.15	0.95	3.05	0.96
Early parenting and caregiving risk factors				
Nonmaternal child care	0.02	0.77	−0.03	0.80
Father's involvement	2.98	1.14	2.27	1.31
Interparental conflict	2.23	0.98	2.20	1.00
Exposure to violence	1.76	1.06	1.76	1.08
Harsh discipline	2.76	0.88	2.58	0.86
Physical abuse	1.56	0.62	1.51	0.65
Positive parenting	3.31	0.65	3.30	0.67
Support of aggression	3.04	0.63	2.92	0.56
Early behavior problems				
Internalizing behavior problems	47.8	10.0	48.2	8.8
Externalizing behavior problems	49.8	9.4	50.6	9.2

Table 16. (Contd.)

Predictor	Males (n = 304)		Females (n = 281)	
	Mean	SD	Mean	SD
Early peer experience risk factors				
Social preference	0.00	0.98	0.33	0.92
Peer rejection	0.14	0.35	0.08	0.27
Years rejected	0.43	0.83	0.31	0.70
Adolescent parental risk factors				
Parental supervision (mother report)	4.59	0.39	4.67	0.38
Parental supervision (adolescent report)	2.68	0.27	2.71	0.26
Adolescent peer and context risk factors				
Neighborhood safety	1.95	0.83	2.04	0.87
Peer drug use (mother report)	1.02	0.11	1.02	0.16
Peer drug use (adolescent report)	1.02	0.08	1.01	0.05
Peer group deviance	1.92	0.68	1.81	0.74
Peer group drug use	1.11	0.05	1.18	0.52
Best friend deviance	0.36	0.36	0.25	0.33
Susceptibility to peer pressure	2.73	0.81	2.41	0.76
Peer deviance (teacher report)	1.70	0.92	1.56	0.99
Adolescent substance use by Grade 12	0.515	0.50	0.511	0.50

DISCUSSION

The major finding was that the pattern of correlations in the dynamic cascade model that has been empirically supported here did not differ significantly for males and females. The robustness of the final empirically supported model across males and females is important because it strengthens the generalizability of the overall dynamic cascade model. This robustness should not be misinterpreted as indicating no main effects of gender, nor should it be interpreted as indicating that any single path does not differ by gender. The test is limited to the full model.

Although it would be important to test robustness across ethnic groups, the small sample size for African Americans ($n = 100$ at T1) prohibited a strong empirical test.

A final set of analyses was conducted at the person level. The preceding variable-level analyses are appropriate for testing the hypotheses of the proposed theoretical model, but clinical decisions are usually made at the discrete-person level (Greenberg, Lengua, Coie, Pinderhughes, & CPPRG, 1999). Children are either chosen or not chosen for inclusion in selected preventive interventions. The dynamic cascade model would posit that such decision-making should be contingent on new information at each point in time. That is, based on combined Time-1 child-factor and context-factor problem scores, a child would be selected (or not) for intervention at Time 1. At Time 2, early parent-factor problems would be used to *supplement* the Time-1 factors to identify children. For example, among children who had been identified at Time 1 as being problems, those children who were *also* problems based on the Time-2 factor would continue to be selected. At Time 3, the early behavior problems factor would supplement this decision-making, and so on. Similar logic would identify children who are protected from risk of later substance use.

The goal of these analyses was to classify children based on the predictor variables into problem versus nonproblem groups in order to examine the degree to which the problem group at each point in time is at risk for illicit substance use.

METHOD

Classification of Children

Participants were classified as low or high in problems on each of the seven predictor variables based on a median split of the variable following multiple imputation and averaging of a participant's postimputation score. Next, participants were dichotomized into two groups of *never-users* of illicit substances and *ever-users* of illicit substances, again using averaged postimputation scores. Thus, each participant received eight dichotomous scores for analysis.

RESULTS

Selection Into Cascades

If the seven problem classifications were independent of each other, 2^7 groups ($n = 128$) would result, each with about 4.57 children (585 participants/128 groups = 4.57). However, 21 children were classified into the "fully cascaded group" defined by high problems on every one of the seven variables, a rate that is much higher than expected by chance, $p < .001$. At the other extreme, 28 children were classified into the lowest possible problem group defined by low problems on all seven variables, also higher than expected by chance, $p < .001$.

Risk for Lifetime Substance Use by Groups

In contrast to a population base rate of .51, the fully cascaded group had a significantly higher probability of lifetime substance use, at .91, $p < .001$, and the lowest possible problem group had a significantly lower probability, at .25, $p < .001$. Table 17 lists the number of children ever using illicit substances as a function of the number of problem factors from 0 through 7. The probability of substance use grew linearly as the number of problem factors increased.

Cascading Increment in Risk

Figure 5 employs a decision-tree format to depict the probabilities of substance use across development for the group of children who were initially high in both child-factor and context-factor problems ($n = 152$). This group had a .69 probability of lifetime substance use (in contrast to the population base rate of .51). The cascade is evidenced in further increments

TABLE 17

RELATION BETWEEN NUMBER OF RISK FACTORS AND LIFETIME ILLICIT SUBSTANCE USE

Number of Risk Factors	Number of Children Never Using Illicit Substances	Number of Children Ever Using Illicit Substances (Row %)
0	21	07 (25)
1	40	21 (34)
2	63	34 (35)
3	60	45 (43)
4	43	57 (57)
5	32	72 (69)
6	16	53 (77)
7	02	19 (91)

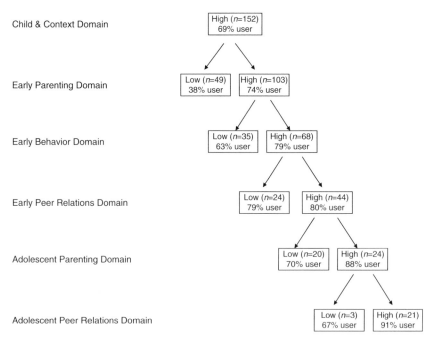

Child & Context Domain — High (n=152) 69% user

Early Parenting Domain — Low (n=49) 38% user | High (n=103) 74% user

Early Behavior Domain — Low (n=35) 63% user | High (n=68) 79% user

Early Peer Relations Domain — Low (n=24) 79% user | High (n=44) 80% user

Adolescent Parenting Domain — Low (n=20) 70% user | High (n=24) 88% user

Adolescent Peer Relations Domain — Low (n=3) 67% user | High (n=21) 91% user

FIGURE 5.—Decision tree for identification of high-risk children at each stage of development.

in the probability of substance use that accrue from high problems at each subsequent stage of development. Among this initially high-problem group, if the next step, early parenting, was also high-problem ($n = 103$), the probability of substance use increased to .74. Among these 103 children, if the next step, early behavior problems, was also high ($n = 68$), the probability increased to .79. Among these 68 children, if the next step, early peer relations problems, was also high ($n = 44$), the probability increased to .80. Among these 44 children, if the next step, adolescent parenting problems, was also high ($n = 24$), the probability increased to .88. Finally, among these 24 children, if the final step, adolescent peer relations, was also high-problem ($n = 21$), the probability increased to .91.

Figure 6 depicts a complementary declining cascade that was evident among the group of children who were initially low in both child-factor and context-factor problems ($n = 151$). This group had a .46 probability of lifetime substance use (in contrast to the population base rate of .51). The declining cascade is evidenced in further decrements in the probability of substance use that accrue from high problems at each subsequent step. Among this initially low-problem group, if the next step, early parenting, was also low-problem ($n = 103$), the probability of substance use decreased

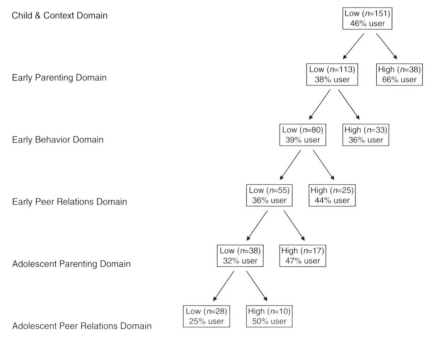

Child & Context Domain

Early Parenting Domain

Early Behavior Domain

Early Peer Relations Domain

Adolescent Parenting Domain

Adolescent Peer Relations Domain

FIGURE 6.—Decision tree for identification of low-risk children at each stage of development.

to .38. Among these 103 children, if the next step, early behavior problems, was also low (*n* = 80), the probability stayed at .39. Among these 80 children, if the next step, early peer relations problems, was also low (*n* = 55), the probability decreased to .36. Among these 55 children, if the next step, adolescent parenting problems, was also low (*n* = 38), the probability decreased to .32. Finally, among these 38 children, if the final step, adolescent peer relations, was also low-problem (*n* = 28), the probability decreased to .25.

DISCUSSION

The findings indicate the dramatic effect of classification on the prediction of later substance use. In contrast with a base rate of 51%, children who followed the entire seven-step developmental cascade had a 91% chance of becoming a substance user, and children who followed none of the seven steps had just a 25% chance of becoming a substance user. These large differences indicate that high-risk children can be identified with high accuracy on the basis of the developmental cascade. Such precise identification improves the likelihood that an efficacious preventive intervention would prove cost-beneficial, because relatively few false positives would be targeted for unnecessary intervention.

The findings also indicate that prediction is improved with each advancing step, from a 69% chance at Time 1 based on child and context factors alone, to a 74% chance after adding the early parenting factor, and so on. Thus, although high-risk youths can be identified early in life, improved prediction occurs with advancing age, consistent with a cascade model.

In a complementary way, these findings indicate the optimistic possibility that high-risk children can be moved off of a cascading path if environmental factors ensue. Thus, for example, among children who were at high risk (69% chance) on the basis of child and context factors, those children who received high-quality early parenting were immediately reduced to just 38% chance. Also, protection against the risk of substance use was improved with positive experiences at each step of the cascade (except for the early behavior domain, which had no effect on reducing risk among those already at relatively low risk, see Figure 5). Whether the protection can also occur through life experiences that are engineered through preventive intervention remains an open question, but these findings point toward the domains that might be targeted in such intervention.

An alternate model to the cascade is a strict child-effects model that posits that risk is determined solely by child factors and that any apparent environmental effects are epiphenomenal to child effects. Given the control variable of early child behavior, this model is rejected in favor of models that posit incremental roles for environmental events across development. It remains plausible, however, that other early child behavior variables might be identified that would yield stronger predictive power.

A second alternate model is Rutter and Garmezy's (1983) cumulative risk model, which posits that risk increments with an increasing number of risk factors without regard to which factor is implicated. Indeed, the findings listed in Table 17 are consistent with a hypothesis of linear increase in risk as a function of number of risk factors. However, the cascade model affords more timely prediction and identification of high-risk children than waiting until all factors can be measured in early adolescence.

In sum, the person-level analyses are consistent with the variable-level analyses in demonstrating the increment in prediction from factors in the cascade model. These analyses go beyond the variable-level analyses by demonstrating the potential value in identifying children at high risk for preventive intervention.

XIII. THEORETICAL INTEGRATION AND DISCUSSION

EMPIRICAL FINDINGS THAT CHARACTERIZE THE DYNAMIC CASCADE

The major findings of this study are summarized in Table 18 and Figure 6. Five patterns support a dynamic cascade model of how substance-use behavior develops across childhood and adolescence, and they also characterize the general features of a dynamic cascade.

First, numerous variables at different times across development each significantly predict the problem outcome, the onset of adolescent substance use. These empirical correlations are consistent with the literature cited in the introduction, which supports the broad hypothesis that adolescent substance use is multiply determined. The question remains whether there exist multiple unique paths to this outcome (i.e., multifinality) or these factors overlap. The problem is not that adolescent maladjustment is unpredictable; the problem is that too many variables, including ones that are probably spurious or endogenous to developmental processes, predict maladjustment outcomes.

Second, predictor variables in socialization generally interrelate significantly in a web of correlations. This pattern was found in the current study, as depicted in Figure 3, and the pattern presents a conundrum in discerning developmental pathways. Seeming pathways that have been identified in prior studies might represent merely selection effects into certain kinds of life experiences, and experiences at each era of life might not represent true increments in the prediction of outcomes. Most previous research has used some form of regression analysis that statistically controls other factors to identify unique prediction, such as the cumulative effects model that was first suggested by Rutter and Garmezy (1983). But the cumulative effects model fails to explain the pattern of intercorrelations across predictor variables, nor the relevance of temporal ordering of relations. The dynamic cascade model and the current method of testing pathways represent novel ways of sorting through the web of intercorrelations and understanding this development.

The third empirical pattern that is characteristic of a dynamic cascade (and found here) is that each succeeding step in development is predictable

TABLE 18

SUMMARY OF MAJOR FINDINGS

Predictor Domain (x)	Does x Predict Substance Use?	Does x Mediate Effect of $x-1$ on Substance Use, Fully or Partially?	Does x Increment $x-1$ in Predicting Substance Use?	Does x Predict $x+2$?	Does x Mediate Effect of $x-1$ on $x+1$, Fully or Partially?	Does x Increment $x-1$ in Predicting $x+2$?
Child factors	Yes	NA	NA	NA	NA	NA
Ecological factors	Yes					
Early parenting	Yes	Full	Yes	Yes	Full	Yes
Conduct problems	Yes	Partial	Yes	Yes	Partial	Yes
Early peers	Yes	Full	Yes	Yes	Full	Yes
Later parenting	Yes	Full	Yes	Yes	Full	Yes
Later peers	Yes	Full	Yes	NA	NA	NA

from the previous step. This pattern represents the continuity in adaptation across development and domains of social life that is familiar to scholars of social development (Cairns & Cairns, 1994; Horowitz, 1987). Cross-time correlations are strongest at points closest to each other in time, but significant correlations extend at least two steps in the developmental chain.

In the current study, patterns in early parenting follow from the social ecology and biological temperament of the child. Parents are likely to have difficulty parenting in a context of stress and disadvantage. In turn, early dysfunctional parenting predicts the child's conduct problem behavior. When the child enters school, previous conduct problems predict problems in peer relations, especially peer social rejection and low social preference. The pattern is reciprocal, in that the child's problems in relating to peers predict a subsequent pattern in which parents alter their monitoring and supervision patterns in early adolescence. Unfortunately, rather than these processes being self-correcting, they seem to be self-exacerbating. The pattern is consistent with the hypothesis that, rather than responding to a child who displays conduct problems and problems in relating to peers by increasing supervision and monitoring, parents respond by withdrawing their supervision, perhaps to ease the overt conflict that ensues from discussions about school conduct problems. In turn, low parental supervision during adolescence predicts a subsequent pattern in which the adolescent associates with deviant peers, which is the final step toward onset of substance use.

The fourth finding is that each succeeding step in a dynamic cascade is not only predictable from the preceding step, but it also significantly mediates the previous step in predicting both the next step in development and the outcome of adolescent substance use. Each succeeding step provides not only a statistical path from the preceding step to long-term outcomes but also suggests a developmental understanding of how preceding factors operate to lead to later outcomes.

In the current study, early parenting behavior that is predictable from a child's social ecology accounts for (part of) the impact of the social ecology on the child's subsequent conduct problems and, ultimately, adolescent substance use. Conduct problems that are predictable from early parenting behavior account for, and describe, how early parenting leads to the child's development of peer relations problems and adolescent substance use. In turn, peer relations problems account for the impact of prior conduct problems on adolescent parenting and substance use. Adolescent parenting difficulty, in turn, accounts for the effect of previous peer relations problems on later substance use. Associating with deviant peers is predicted from inadequate parenting during adolescence, accounts for the effect of inadequate parenting on substance use, and represents the final step toward the youth's onset of substance use.

The fifth empirical finding is that each succeeding step significantly increments the prediction afforded by the previous step. This finding indicates that the ultimate path is not fully determined by the first step. Rather, each step adds unique information in propelling a child toward or away from substance use.

The net outcome of the pattern of developmental mediation with unique increments at each step is a dynamic cascade. In the current study, this parsimonious model (depicted in Figure 4) describes how substance use develops from early childhood through adolescence. The web of correlations among socializing variables can be reduced to a much smaller set that provides a more concise statistical prediction and a more parsimonious understanding of how adolescent outcomes grow out of early life experiences.

IMPLICATIONS OF THE DYNAMIC CASCADE FOR THEORIES OF SOCIAL DEVELOPMENT

Six aspects of the empirical findings have implications for theories of social development in many domains: (1) multiple modest effects; (2) the primacy of early influences; (3) continuity in adaptation; (4) reciprocal transactional development; (5) nonlinear growth in problem behaviors during sensitive periods; and (6) new opportunities for change with each new domain over time.

Multiple Modest Effects

No single correlation predicting adolescent substance use had a "strong" effect size, but many correlations reached conventional levels of statistical significance. Social development in many domains (e.g., aggression, Greenberg et al., 1999) is characterized by multiple, small-magnitude influences on outcomes, whether these influences are multiple socializing effects, multiple biological effects, or a combination (Horowitz, 1987). Like tiny streams that merge into a rushing river, the accumulation of these small effects, however, is enormous.

The Primacy of Early Influences

The current findings indicate the primacy of early influences, not because they are larger in magnitude than later effects but because they trigger cascades that grow into larger effects across time. Simply because they come first, while the rest of development remains a blank slate, early influences have inordinate power to shape later outcomes. They determine early vectors of development, like early streams that cascade downstream into powerful forces. Although plasticity remains across all stages of development, the magnitude of plasticity decreases with each advancing age (Shonkoff & Phillips, 2000).

Continuity in Adaptation

The current findings indicate continuity in adaptation across long periods in time, even with discontinuity of behavior (Cairns & Cairns, 1994). Early conduct problems predict adolescent substance use, even though these behaviors are very different in their form and, perhaps, even function. Furthermore, the current study provides evidence of continuity of socializing environments, even if the active forces of socialization change across development. In early childhood, the active parenting forces include discipline strategies, whereas in adolescence the forces include parents' monitoring and supervision. These very different socializing behaviors are empirically continuous. In early childhood, the active peer forces derive from peers' social acceptance or rejection of the child, whereas in adolescence peer group cliques provide the ground for socialization. These peer factors are also very different but empirically related.

Although these socializing forces are very different across time, the sources of influence remain the same (albeit the strength of influence may change across domains). An important point is the evidence for continuity in the adaptiveness of the socializing environment, although the environment itself may change and the precise form of influences may change dramatically.

Reciprocal Transactional Development

The current findings support Sameroff's (2009) concept of transactional development. This concept posits that the self interacts with the environment to produce an impact on the environment, which, in turn, reciprocates by influencing the self. The concept goes beyond reciprocal influences because each force alters the other in a way that characterizes a transaction. Sameroff and Mackenzie (2003) noted the methodological difficulties in empirically testing the concepts of transactional development because of the large number of endogenous influences that are posited across development. The current study provides a methodology for studying these influences and numerous empirical findings of transactional influences across several domains. Not only does the child influence peers to accept or reject him or her, but also the peer group later influences the youth's onset of substance use. Not only does the early parent influence the child's development of conduct problems through discipline strategies and parent–child warmth, but also the child influences the later parent to withdraw from monitoring and supervision, either to ease the conflict or through the child's deviousness. Even socializing forces transact with each other. Parents influence the peer group (indirectly through their influence on child behavior), and the peer group influences the parent (to alter monitoring). The entire network of socializing forces can be characterized as transacting across development.

Nonlinear Growth in Problem Behaviors During Sensitive Periods

Like Granic and Patterson's (2006) dynamic systems model of antisocial behavioral development, a dynamic cascade model posits nonlinear acceleration of problem behaviors during critical periods in development and emergence of new problem behaviors, such as substance use. Dynamic models posit and explain state transitions, such as the change from child whining to peer-directed aggression. In the current study, the child's state change is from conduct problems to substance use, and then rapid acceleration in substance-use onset, during the adolescent period.

Accelerating growth and state transitions occur partially because of the accumulation of factors, but also through the transactions that occur across domains, rendering certain socializing forces even more powerful over time, and the confluence of socializing factors with the youth's biological readiness. It is not merely a coincidence that substance use grows rapidly during adolescence. Adolescence is a discrete period in life characterized biologically by increases in sensitivity to rewarding sensations. The reward system (also known as the *behavioral activation system*), which is primarily guided by the nucleus accumbens and limbic centers, facilitates the active search for reward. Activation of these centers transforms motivational drives into behavioral actions (Panksepp, 1998). This system is biologically immature as individuals emerge from childhood, and there is evidence that it reaches its greatest tonic activity level during adolescence (Ernst, Pine, & Hardin, 2005).

Reward sensitivity heightens the risk for substance use. Animal behavioral experiments have repeatedly indicated the critical sensitivity of adolescent rodents to become users and abusers of cocaine (Caster, Walker, & Kuhn, 2005), alcohol (Little, Kuhn, Wilson, & Swartzwelder, 1996), and nicotine (Levin, Rezvani, Montoya, Rose, & Swartzwelder, 2003) during the few days of their adolescence. So, too, compared with their adult counterparts, human adolescents are more likely to engage in drunk driving, unprotected sex, illicit drug use, and minor criminal activities (Arnett, 1992) and less likely to precontemplate potential aversive outcomes of risky behavior (Tangney et al., 1996). But adolescence itself is never sufficient as an explanation for substance-use onset. Adolescents interact in a social environment. Only in confluence with the myriad ecological and socializing forces does substance use begin during adolescence.

New Opportunities for Change With Each Transition

A paradox of the dynamic cascade model is that with each advancing age or transition, there exist both decreasing plasticity and new opportunities for change in adaptation. The decreasing plasticity occurs as neural pathways become well set. The new opportunities come about because a new domain does not merely transmit the effects of the previous domain in a passive manner; the new domain exerts new impact, which, by definition, implies the statistical likelihood that exogenous forces will exert a change in the equilibrium of the system. That is, each new domain of development represents an opportunity for changing the "set" of seemingly inevitable development. With new stimuli, there is a new main-effect impact on the youth's development.

The paradox lies in the fact that, even though new stimuli exert new effects on development in ways that are independent from all previous factors, youths are differentially exposed to these new stimuli because of the continuity of adaptation and biased selection into certain experiences. Previous domains exert some of their impact by exposing a youth to a biased set of stimuli in the next domain of development. Not all youths are equally likely to be exposed to a particular stimulus. Previous life experiences bias some youths toward or away from exposure to subsequent life events, even

97

if those events have an impact. Thus, as an example, although high parental monitoring during early adolescence exerts a new impact on tilting a child away from substance-use development, previous life experiences bias some families away from imposing monitoring, thus limiting the actual impact that this new life experience has on youth outcomes. Unfortunately, those youths who are at greatest risk for substance use and might benefit most from high parental monitoring during early adolescence are least likely to receive this experience.

Each new developmental domain offers both opportunity and risk. Opportunity lies in the possibility that a youth who has been headed toward substance use can be deflected in this trajectory by a new life experience. Following the example above, a child who has displayed conduct problems and peer social rejection can change vectors through exposure to a parent who decides to impose high levels of monitoring and supervision. Goodnight, Bates, Pettit, and Dodge (2008) found that when parents initiate a "campaign" to change their child's deviant behavior through concerted efforts, the child's behavior can, indeed, improve. These opportunities occur naturally through the random walk of life but also systematically through intervention. The "random walk" can also impose a new risk, however. Thus, the child who has not displayed conduct problems and has been accepted by peers during childhood might still be shifted toward substance use if the parents do not monitor and supervise the youth during early adolescence.

IMPLICATIONS FOR PREVENTIVE INTERVENTION DESIGN

The findings indicate that children who are at risk for adolescent substance use can be identified in early life, and they suggest that factors that are present in early life (e.g., social ecology of disadvantage, early problems in parenting behavior) may play pivotal roles in charting some children on a trajectory toward adolescent problem behavior. These findings suggest that preventive interventions that are targeted toward early risk factors might prove successful in reducing risk for substance use.

Because high-risk children and relevant risk factors can be identified by school entry, this era might be a logical place to initiate preventive intervention, with a goal of cost-effective pay-off by deflecting trajectories of deviant development (Conduct Problems Prevention Research Group, 1992). At this point in life, parenting dysfunction can be assessed and changed (Patterson, Reid, & Dishion, 1992) through evidence-based interventions. Policies to reduce early family poverty and stress might yield long-term dividends (Isaacs, 2007). However, these interventions are likely to be insufficient. New risks present themselves across development, and so intervention might well need to occur later in adolescence. One implication of the current findings is that although early intervention might have wide-reaching effects, the concept of early immunization against long-term adverse outcomes must be dispelled because later risks emerge and because feasible time-limited interventions cannot actually remove all the risks or provide all the relevant skills. In deciding whether to intervene in early childhood or adolescence, intervention designers must trade the cascading benefits of early identification and intervention with the costs of relatively high rates of false-positive and false-negative identification if screening occurs early in childhood. Likewise, a decision to wait until adolescence to initiate intervention involves a trade-off between the benefits of more accurate identification of high-risk youths and the increased challenge of intervening after the cascade has accelerated deviant development and may be more difficult to interrupt. One solution is sustained intervention across childhood and adolescence, but such an approach may prove costly and difficult to achieve.

Yet another question for intervention design is whether to target universally with all children in a population versus selectively with high-risk youths only (Tolan & Dodge, 2005). Aspects of these findings suggest that targeting high-risk youths is possible and could provide individualized focus to intervene in domains of difficulty for a particular child. On the other hand, some domains that have been identified here reflect environmental factors (e.g., early social ecology of disadvantage, the tendency for a peer culture to reject an aggressive child, the ease with which deviant youths are able to find deviant peer groups with which to associate) that may be impossible to change by working with a small number of individuals. Greater success might accrue through systemic change at the universal, or even policy, level (Dodge, 2007).

A solution that balances early and later identification and universal versus selected intervention can be borrowed from the model of education to prevent illiteracy (Dodge, 2007). In the United States, universal education is mandated for all children from age 5 (or 7 in some locales) to age 16 (or 18). Special education is provided for selected children who have been screened to be at high risk for poor outcomes. At each age, new curricular material is presented to each child, and new screening occurs to select specific high-risk children for placement into special education. This policy has features of both universal and selected intervention, and it spans childhood and adolescence. It recognizes that new tasks are deemed relevant at each age and new risks confront children as they get older. The empirical findings of the current study suggest that such a plan must be developed to prevent youths from substance use in adolescence.

The findings have important implications for understanding the economic benefits that might accrue from early interventions. Isaacs (2007), for example, has used findings from past early intervention evaluations to argue that investment in early intervention reaps benefits at over 16% per annum. Heckman and Masterov (2006) also call for investments in early life, buttressing their economic argument in favor of early intervention by conjecturing that the reason that early intervention is so effective is that "skill begets skill" (p. 3).

The empirical sequences identified in the current study describe the cascade of how early deficits grow over time to other deficits in other domains. But the current analysis also indicates that early intervention is not sufficient. That is, new risks arise across development, threatening all children, whether or not they had received early intervention previously. Later intervention is likely necessary to supplement the impact of early intervention.

The current findings give empirical support for the economic simulations by Cunha and Heckman (2006), who reached a similar conclusion. They utilized data from economically disadvantaged women who were part of the National Longitudinal Study of Youth, 1979 cohort, who had become mothers of boys, to estimate the likely returns on investments in these boys at various ages. They found that with no additional investment, only 41% would graduate from high school, 4% would enroll in college, 23% would be convicted of crimes, and 18% would be on welfare rolls. They then simulated the impact on these outcomes if these children had received a comprehensive preschool program. They estimated that high school graduation rates for this population of boys would jump to 66%, college enrollment would increase to 13%, criminal convictions would decrease to 17%, and welfare dependency would fall to 9%. If these boys were to receive skill-building investments during their adolescent years on top of the preschool investments, estimated graduation rates would rise to 85%, and college enrollment would rise to 27%. Criminal convictions would drop to 13%, and welfare dependency would drop to 4%. Finally, they estimated that a comprehensive investment that was sustained across early childhood, middle childhood, and adolescence would yield the best outcomes: 91% high school graduation, 38% college enrollment, only 11% criminal convictions, and 3% welfare dependency. These simulations suggest that although early intervention improves adolescent and adult outcomes, later interventions at various points across childhood supplement the improvement in cost-beneficial ways.

A critique of the study by America's Promise (2007) concluded that "(i)nvestments also accumulate over time. Thus, skills at a later stage build on the skills of a previous stage, which leads to more productive overall investments . . . Because later skills build off of previous skills, Heckman and Cunha theorize that continued investments at all stages of a child's development will pay greater dividends than those that are concentrated on discrete periods; for example, investments made only during early childhood will be less productive than investments started in early childhood and continued throughout middle childhood and adolescence" (p. 46). Such is the nature of a dynamic cascade.

Economists estimate the benefits of these positive outcomes as being huge. Lochner and Moretti (2004), for example, estimate that a 1% increase in high school graduation rates nationwide would yield US$1.8 billion in social benefits and reduce the number of crimes nationwide by 94,000. The current study suggests that some of this benefit would likely accrue from successful early interventions, but the actual savings might be overstated due to overlap in predictors and outcomes. Although Cohen (1998, 2005) estimates the lifetime cost per adolescent persistent drug abuser at US$970,000 and the lifetime cost of a chronically violent adolescent at over US$2 million, the current study suggests that estimates must have wide confidence intervals because of high intercorrelation among problem-behavior outcomes as well as high intercorrelation among developmental risk factors for these outcomes. Because early conduct problems predict adolescent early-onset substance use, it is not clear whether or not the ultimate cost of these individuals sums the lifetime costs of each problem or discounts overlapping problems.

LIMITS AND CAVEATS

The limits of this study are important to note. The first limit is that the data are correlational and therefore subject to alternate interpretations of selection biases and unmeasured third-variable causation. It is plausible that what appears in the current study as an incremental effect of a new domain on outcomes (e.g., adolescent parenting increments the impact of previous domains in predicting substance-use onset) is actually merely self-selection into that domain through a factor that has not been measured. Statistical control from the measured variables does not preclude self-selection from unmeasured third variables. Future research must identify plausible third variables and control for them statistically. Better yet would intervention experiments in which change in a domain is engineered through systematic intervention, and cascading effects are observed.

A second limit is that the current study addressed only substance-use onset and not substance abuse or substance-use disorder. The focus here

101

was on early-onset substance use because it is not normative and has been linked to long-term serious outcomes (Clark & Winters, 2002). It is plausible, however, that different pathways to these serious outcomes may be identified.

A third limit concerns the plausibility of alternate developmental models of substance-use onset. Here we were constrained by the variables that had been assessed in the Child Development Project. It is plausible, even likely, that other unmeasured variables would contribute both to enriched estimates within identified domains of development and additional domains. Certainly, the domain of child factors could be enriched by measurement of genetic variables, and the social–ecological domain could be enriched by better measurement of family stress and income. A more complete model could identify additional domains that could be measured temporally in between measured domains. For example, academic success likely plays a role in mediating the chain between early poor peer relations and adolescent parental monitoring. Yet greater enrichment would accrue from consideration of transactional iterations between two adjoining domains. The relation between child conduct problems and peer social rejection, for example, has been found to be iterative, such that each domain leads to increments in the other domain (Dodge et al., 2003).

We considered testing alternate models using the variables in the current study but were constrained by temporally impossible causal chains (e.g., adolescent parenting cannot lead to early poor peer relations). The models tested in Chapter X are meant to represent plausible alternatives. Still other models could be tested in future studies.

Finally, the cascade concept implies that temporally later environmental inputs will have more proximal influence on outcomes than temporally precedent inputs. Thus, the findings are also consistent with the benign hypothesis that later factors always mediate earlier factors, no matter what they are. We could have tested theoretically inconsistent models to refute that notion (e.g., we could test the implausible hypothesis that adolescent socioeconomic status mediates the impact of early peer relations on substance-use outcomes), but the exercise seemed meaningless because, no matter what the outcome, it would not truly refute the general point that plausible developmental pathways are also temporally constrained.

FUTURE RESEARCH

The findings reported here and the concept of a dynamic cascade suggest avenues for future inquiry. We believe that two kinds of longitudinal studies will complement each other. One kind concerns short-term developmental chains (e.g., how early parenting leads to poor peer relations). Most past research has been of this kind. These studies address the mediation of a single pathway over a relatively short period of time by a single hypothesized mediator. These studies provide the building blocks for the second kind of longitudinal study, which concerns multistep chains over long periods of development. Because these multiple steps accelerate development of problem behaviors and account for the impact of a wide array of variables across long periods of development, we call them dynamic cascades. Future tests of dynamic cascades should continue to borrow from previous short-term findings (as the current study did), and tests of dynamic cascades should suggest gaps in knowledge of short-term processes that could be addressed in future short-term studies.

The concept of a dynamic cascade could well be applied to other behaviors, including both problems and successes, such as high school graduation, adolescent pregnancy, and the acquisition of sexually transmitted diseases such as HIV. Different variables and domains would surely be relevant, because different developmental theory and processes would apply. But the concepts of a dynamic cascade might well prove useful in understanding the development of these outcomes across childhood and adolescence.

REFERENCES

Achenbach, T. M. (1991). *Manual for the youth self report form and 1991 profile*. Burlington: University of Vermont.

Achenbach, T. M., & Edelbrock, C. S. (1986). *Manual for the teacher's report form and teacher version of the child behavior profile*. Burlington: University of Vermont.

Allison, K. W., Crawford, I., Leone, P. E., Trickett, E., Perez-Febles, A., Burton, L. M., et al. (1999). Adolescent substance use: Preliminary examinations of school and neighborhood context. *American Journal of Community Psychology*, **27**, 111–134.

America's Promise. (2007). *Every child, every promise: Turning failure into action*. Retrieved from http://www.americaspromise.org

Armstrong, T. D., & Costello, E. J. (2002). Community studies on adolescent substance use, abuse, or dependence and psychiatric comorbidity. *Journal of Consulting and Clinical Psychology*, **70**, 1224–1239.

Arnett, J. (1992). The soundtrack of recklessness: Musical preferences and reckless behavior among adolescents. *Journal of Adolescent Research*, **7**, 313–331.

Bachman, J. G., Lloyd, D. J., & O'Malley, P. M. (1981). Smoking, drinking, and drug use among American high school students: Correlates and trends, 1975–1979. *American Journal of Public Health*, **71**, 59–69.

Bagwell, C. L., Coie, J. D., Terry, R. A., & Lochman, J. E. (2000). Peer clique participation in middle childhood: Associations with sociometric status and gender. *Merrill-Palmer Quarterly*, **46**, 280–305.

Barnes, G. M., Reifman, A. S., Farrell, M. P., & Dintcheff, B. A. (2000). The effects of parenting on the development of adolescent alcohol misuse: A six-wave latent growth model. *Journal of Marriage and the Family*, **62**, 175–186.

Barnes, G. M., & Welte, J. W. (1986). Patterns and predictors of alcohol use among 7–12th grade students in New York State. *Journal of Studies on Alcohol*, **47**, 53–62.

Bates, J. E., & Bayles, K. (1984). Objective and subjective components in mothers' perceptions of their children from age 6 months to 3 years. *Merrill-Palmer Quarterly*, **30**, 111–130.

Bates, J. E., Freeland, C. B., & Lounsbury, M. L. (1979). Measurement of infant difficultness. *Child Development*, **50**, 794–803.

Bates, J. E., Marvinney, D., Kelly, T., Dodge, K. A., Bennett, D. S., & Pettit, G. S. (1994). Child care history and kindergarten adjustment. *Developmental Psychology*, **30**, 690–700.

Baumrind, D. (1983, October). *Why adolescents take chances—And why they don't*. Paper presented at the National Institute for Child Health and Human Development, Bethesda, MD.

Baumrind, D. (1985). Familial antecedents of adolescent drug use: A developmental perspective. In C. L. Jones & R. J. Battjes (Eds.), *Etiology of drug abuse: Implications for prevention* (pp. 13–44). Rockville, MD: National Institute on Drug Abuse.

Benjet, C., & Kazdin, A. E. (2003). Spanking children: The controversies, findings, and new directions. *Clinical Psychology Review*, **23**, 197–224.

Beyers, J. M., Bates, J. E., Pettit, G. S., & Dodge, K. A. (2003). Neighborhood structure, parenting processes, and the development of youths' externalizing behaviors: A multilevel analysis. *American Journal of Community Psychology*, **31**, 35–53.

Block, J., Block, J. H., & Keyes, S. (1988). Longitudinally foretelling mental precursors. *Child Development*, **59**, 336–355.

Bogenschneider, K., Wu, M. Y., Raffaelli, M., & Tsay, J. C. (1998). Parent influences on adolescent peer orientation and substance use: The interface of parenting practices and values. *Child Development*, **69**, 1672–1688.

Boker, S. M., & Graham, J. W. (1998). A dynamical systems analysis of adolescent substance use. *Multivariate Behavioral Research*, **33**(4), 479–507.

Bollen, K. A., & Stine, R. A. (1992). Bootstrapping goodness-of-fit measures in structural equation models. *Sociological Methods and Research*, **21**, 205–229.

Botvin, G. J. (1986). Substance abuse prevention research: Recent developments and future directions. *Journal of School Health*, **56**, 369–374.

Bowman, B. P., & Kuhn, C. M. (1996). Age-related differences in the chronic and acute response to cocaine in the rat. *Developmental Psychobiology*, **29**(97–611).

Boyle, M. H., Offord, D. R., Racine, Y. A., Szatmari, P., Fleming, J. E., & Links, P. (1992). Predicting substance use in late adolescence: Results of the Ontario Child Health Study follow-up. *American Journal of Psychiatry*, **149**, 761–767.

Bray, J. H., Adams, G. J., Getz, J., & McQueen, A. (2003). Individuation, peers, and adolescent alcohol use: A latent growth analysis. *Journal of Consulting and Clinical Psychology*, **71**, 553–555.

Brody, G. H., Ge, X., Katz, J., & Arias, I. (2000). A longitudinal analysis of internalization of parental alcohol-use norms and adolescent alcohol use. *Applied Developmental Science*, **4**, 71–79.

Brook, J. S., Brook, D. W., Gordon, A. S., Whiteman, M., & Cohen, P. (1990). The psychosocial etiology of adolescent drug use: A family interactional approach. *Genetic, Social, and General Psychology Monographs*, **116**, 111–267.

Brook, J. S., Gordon, A. S., Whiteman, M., & Cohen, P. (1986). Some models and mechanisms for explaining the impact of maternal and adolescent characteristics on adolescent stage of drug use. *Developmental Psychology*, **22**, 460–467.

Brown, G. G., Mounts, N., Lamborn, S. D., & Steinberg, L. (1993). Parenting practices and peer group affiliation in adolescence. *Child Development*, **64**, 467–482.

Buss, A., & Plomin, R. (1984). *Temperament: Early developing personality traits*. Hillsdale, NJ: Erlbaum.

Cadoret, R. J., Cain, C. A., & Grove, W. M. (1980). Development of alcoholism in adoptees raised apart from alcoholic biologic relatives. *Archives of General Psychiatry*, **37**, 561–563.

Cairns, R. B., & Cairns, B. D. (1994). *Lifelines and risks: Pathways of youth in our time*. New York: Cambridge University Press.

Capaldi, D. M., Dishion, T. J., Stoolmiller, M., & Yoerger, K. (2001). Aggression toward female partners by at-risk young men: The contribution of male adolescent friendships. *Developmental Psychology*, **37**, 61–73.

Capaldi, D. M., & Patterson, G. R. (1989). *Psychometric properties of fourteen latent constructs from the Oregon Youth Study*. New York: Springer-Verlag.

Caprara, G. V., Dodge, K. A., Pastorelli, C., & Zelli, A. (2007). How marginal deviations sometimes grow into serious aggression. *Child Development Perspectives*, **1**, 33–39.

Caprara, G. V., Dodge, K. A., Pastorelli, C., Zelli, A, & Conduct Problems Prevention Research Group. (2006). The effects of marginal deviations on behavioral development. *European Psychologist 2006*, **11**(2), 79–89.

Caster, J. M., Walker, Q. D., & Kuhn, C. M. (2005). Enhanced behavioral response to cocaine in adolescent rats. *Psychopharmacology*, **183**, 218–225.

Catalano, R. F., Kosterman, R., Hawkins, J. D., Newcomb, M. D., & Abbott, R. D. (1996). Modeling the etiology of adolescent substance use: A test of the social development model. *Journal of Drug Issues*, **26**, 429–455.

Caulkins, J. P., Reuter, P. H., Iguchi, M. Y., & Chiesa, J. (2005). *Assessing U.S. drug problems and policy: A synthesis of the evidence to date*. RAND Research Briefs No. RB-9110-DPRC.

Chassin, L., Curran, P. J., Hussong, A. M., & Colder, C. R. (1996). The relation of parent alcoholism to adolescent substance use: A longitudinal follow-up study. *Journal of Abnormal Psychology*, **105**, 70–80.

Chassin, L., Flora, D., & King, K. (2004). Trajectories of alcohol and drug use and dependence from adolescence to adulthood: The effects of familial alcoholism and personality. *Journal of Abnormal Psychology*, **113**, 577–595.

Chilcoat, H. D., & Anthony, J. C. (1996). Impact of parent monitoring on initiation of drug use through late childhood. *Journal of the American Academy of Child Adolescent Psychiatry*, **35**, 91–100.

Chin, W. W. (1998). The partial least squares approach to structural equation modeling. In G. A. Marcoulides (Ed.), *Modern methods for business research* (pp. 295–336). Mahwah, NJ: Lawrence Erlbaum.

Cillessen, A. H. N., & Mayeux, L. (2004). From censure to reinforcement: Developmental changes in the association between aggression and social status. *Child Development*, **75**, 147–163.

Clark, D. B., Lesnick, L., & Hegedus, A. M. (1997). Traumas and other adverse life events in adolescents with alcohol abuse and dependence. *Journal of the American Academy of Child and Adolescent Psychiatry*, **36**, 1744–1751.

Clark, D. B., Parker, A. M., & Lynch, K. G. (1999). Psychopathology and substance-related problems during early adolescence: A survival analysis. *Journal of Clinical Child Psychology*, **28**, 333–341.

Clark, D. B., & Winters, K. C. (2002). Measuring risks and outcomes in substance use disorders prevention research. *Journal of Consulting and Clinical Psychology*, **70**, 1207–1223.

Cloninger, C. R. (1986). A unified biosocial theory of personality and its role in the development of anxiety states. *Psychiatric Developments*, **3**, 167–226.

Cloninger, C. R. (1987). Neurogenetic adaptive mechanisms in alcoholism. *Science*, **236**, 410–416.

Cloninger, C. R., Bohman, M., Sigvardsson, S., & von Knorring, A. L. (1985). Psychopathology in adopted-out children of alcoholics: The Stockholm Adoption Study. *Recent Developments in Alcoholism*, **3**, 37–51.

Cloninger, C. R., Sigvardsson, S., & Bohman, M. (1988). Childhood personality predicts alcohol abuse in young adults. *Alcoholism*, **12**, 494–503.

Cohen, M. A. (1998). Monetary value of saving a high-risk youth. *Journal of Quantitative Criminology*, **24**, 5–33.

Cohen, M. A. (2005). *The costs of crime and justice*. New York: Routledge.

Coie, J. D., & Dodge, K. A. (1983). Continuity of children's social status: A five year longitudinal study. *Merrill-Palmer Quarterly*, **29**, 261–282.

Coie, J. D., Dodge, K. A., & Coppotelli, H. (1982). Dimensions and types of social status: A cross-age perspective. *Developmental Psychology*, **18**, 557–570.

Cole, D. A. (2006). Coping with longitudinal data in research on developmental psychopathology. *International Journal of Behavioral Development*, **30**, 20–25.

Cole, D. A., & Maxwell, S. E. (2003). Testing mediational models with longitudinal data: Myths and tips in the use of structural equation modeling. *Journal of Abnormal Psychology*, **112**, 558–577.

Collins, W. A., Maccoby, E., Steinberg, L., Hetherington, E. M., & Bornstein, M. (2000). Contemporary research on parenting: The case for nature and nurture. *American Psychologist*, **55**, 218–232.

Conduct Problems Prevention Research Group. (1992). A developmental and clinical model for the prevention of conduct disorders: The FAST Track Program. *Development and Psychopathology*, **4**, 509–527.

Costa, F. M., Jessor, R., & Turbin, M. S. (1999). Transition into adolescent problem drinking: The role of psychosocial risk and protective factors. *Journal of Studies on Alcohol*, **60**, 480–490.

Costello, E. J., Erkanli, A., Federman, E., & Angold, A. (1999). Development of psychiatric comorbidity with substance abuse in adolescents: Effects of timing and sex. *Journal of Clinical Child Psychology*, **28**, 298–311.

Culverhouse, R., Bucholz, K. K., Crowe, R. R., Hasselbrock, V., Nurnberger, J. I., Porjesz, B., et al. (2005). Long-term stability of alcohol and other substance dependence diagnoses and habitual smoking. *Archives of General Psychiatry*, **62**, 753–760.

Cunha, F., & Heckman, J. J. (2006). *Investing in our young people. Report prepared for America's Promise—The Alliance for Youth*. Chicago: University of Chicago. Retrieved from: http://www.americaspromise.org

Curran, P. J., Stice, E., & Chassin, L. (1997). The relation between adolescent alcohol use and peer alcohol use: A longitudinal random coefficients model. *Journal of Consulting and Clinical Psychology*, **65**, 130–140.

Dahl, R. E., & Spear, L. P. (2004). Adolescent brain development: Vulnerabilities and opportunities. *Annals of the New York Academy of Sciences*, **1021**, 1–22.

Deater-Deckard, K., Dodge, K. A., Bates, J. E., & Pettit, G. S. (1998). Multiple-risk factors in the development of externalizing behavior problems: Group and individual differences. *Development and Psychopathology*, **10**, 469–493.

Deykin, E. Y., Buka, S. L., & Zeena, T. H. (1992). Depressive illness among chemically dependent adolescents. *American Journal of Psychiatry*, **149**, 1341–1347.

Dick, D. M., Bierut, L., Hinrichs, A., Fox, L., Bucholz, K. K., Kramer, J., et al. (2006). The role of *GABRA2* in risk for conduct disorder and alcohol and drug dependence across developmental stages. *Behavior Genetics*, **36**(4), 577–590.

Dick, D. M., Latendresse, S. J., Lansford, J. E., Budde, J. P., Goate, A., Dodge, K. A., et al. (2009). The role of GABRA2 in trajectories of externalizing behavior across development and evidence of moderation by parental monitoring. *Archives of General Psychiatry*.

Dielman, T. E., Butchart, A. T., Shope, J. T., & Miller, M. (1991). Environmental correlates of adolescent substance use and misuse: Implications for prevention programs. *International Journal of Addictions*, **25**, 855–880.

Dishion, T. J. (2006). Deviant peer contagion within interventions and programs: An ecological framework for understanding influence mechanisms. In K. A. Dodge, T. J. Dishion, & J. E. Lamsford (Eds.), *Deviant peer contagion in therapeutic interventions: From documentation to policy*. New York: Guilford Press.

Dishion, T. J., Capaldi, D., Spracklen, K. M., & Li, F. (1995). Peer ecology of male adolescent drug use. *Development and Psychopathology*, **7**, 803–824.

Dishion, T. J., Capaldi, D. M., & Yoerger, K. (1999). Middle childhood antecedents to progressions in male adolescent substance use: An ecological analysis of risk and protection. *Journal of Adolescent Research*, **14**, 175–205.

Dishion, T. J., & Dodge, K. A. (2006). Deviant peer contagion in interventions and programs: An ecological framework for understanding influence mechanisms. In K. A. Dodge, T. J. Dishion & J. E. Lansford (Eds.), *Deviant peer influences in programs for youth: Problems and solutions* (pp. 14–43). New York: Guilford.

Dishion, T. J., French, D. C., & Patterson, G. R. (1995). The development and ecology of antisocial behavior. In D. Cicchetti & D. J. Cohen (Eds.), *Developmental psychopathology: Vol. 2. Risk, disorder, and adaptation* (pp. 421–471). New York: Wiley.

Dishion, T. J., & Owen, L. D. (2002). A longitudinal analysis of friendships and substance use: Bidirectional influence from adolescence to adulthood. *Developmental Psychology*, **38**, 480–491.

Dishion, T. J., Patterson, G. R., Stoolmiller, M., & Skinner, M. L. (1991). Family, school, and behavioral antecedents to early adolescent involvement with antisocial peers. *Developmental Psychology*, **27**, 172–180.

Disney, E. Y., Elkins, I. J., McGue, M., & Iacono, W. G. (1999). Effects of ADHD, conduct disorder, and gender on substance use and abuse in adolescence. *American Journal of Psychiatry*, **156**, 1515–1521.

Dodge, K. A. (2007). *Strategic framing and the use of metaphors for the prevention of chronic violence in youth.* Manuscript submitted for publication.

Dodge, K. A., Bates, J. E., & Pettit, G. S. (1990). Mechanisms in the cycle of violence. *Science*, **250**, 1678–1683.

Dodge, K. A., Coie, J. D., & Lynam, D. (2006). Aggression and antisocial behavior in youth. In W. Damon (Series Ed.) & N. Eisenberg (Vol. Ed.), *Handbook of child psychology: Vol. 3. Social, emotional, and personality development* (6th ed., pp. 719–788). New York: Wiley.

Dodge, K. A., Greenberg, M. T., Malone, P. S., & the Conduct Problems Prevention Research Group. (2008). Testing an idealized dynamic cascade model of the development of serious violence in adolescence. *Child Development*, **79**, 1907–1927.

Dodge, K. A., & Pettit, G. S. (2003). A biopsychosocial model of the development of chronic conduct problems in adolescence. *Developmental Psychology*, **39**(2), 349–371.

Dodge, K. A., Lansford, J. E., Burks, V. S., Bates, J. E., Pettit, G. S., Fontaine, R., et al. (2003). Peer rejection and social information-processing factors in the development of aggressive behavior problems in children. *Child Development*, **74**, 374–393.

Dodge, K. A., Malone, P. S., Lansford, J. E., Miller-Johnson, S., Pettit, G. S., & Bates, J. E. (2006). Toward a dynamic developmental model of the role of parents and peers in early onset substance use. In A. Clarke-Stewart & J. Dunn (Eds.), *Families count: Effects on child and adolescent development* (pp. 104–134). New York: Cambridge University Press.

Dodge, K. A., Pettit, G. S., & Bates, J. E. (1994a). Socialization mediators of the relation between socioeconomic status and child conduct problems. *Child Development*, **65**, 649–665.

Dodge, K. A., Pettit, G. S., & Bates, J. E. (1994b). Effects of physical maltreatment on the development of peer relations. *Development and Psychopathology*, **6**, 43–55.

Donovan, J. E. (2007). Really underage drinkers: The epidemiology of children's alcohol use in the United States. *Prevention Science*, **8**, 192–205.

Eaton, N. R., Krueger, R. F., Johnson, W., McGue, M., & Iacono, W. G. (2009). Parental monitoring, personality, and delinquency: Further support for a reconceptualization of monitoring. *Journal of Research in Personality*, **43**, 49–59.

Ellickson, P. L., Hays, R. D., & Bell, R. M. (1992). Stepping through the drug use sequence: Longitudinal scalogram analysis of initiation and regular use. *Journal of Abnormal Psychology*, **101**, 441–451.

Elliot, D. S., Huizinga, D., & Ageton, S. S. (1985). *Explaining delinquency and drug use.* Beverly Hills, CA: Sage.

Ennett, S. T., Rosenbaum, D. P., Flewelling, R. L., Biehler, G. S., Ringwalt, C. L., & Bailey, S. L. (1994). Long-term evaluation of drug abuse resistance education. *Addictive Behaviors*, **19**, 113–125.

Ennett, S. T., Ringwalt, C. L., Thorne, J., Rohrbach, L. A., Vincus, A., Simons-Rudolph, A., et al. (2003). A comparison of current practice in school-based substance use prevention programs with meta-analysis findings. *Prevention Science*, **4**, 1–14.

Ernst, M., Pine, D. S., & Hardin, M. (2005). Triadic model of the neurobiology of motivated behavior in adolescence. *Psychological Medicine*, **35**(1–14).

Farmer, E. M. Z., Compton, S. N., Burns, B. J., & Robertson, E. (2002). Review of the evidence base for treatment of childhood psychopathology: Externalizing disorders. *Journal of Consulting and Clinical Psychology*, **70**, 1267–1302.

Farrington, D. P., & Hawkins, J. D. (1991). Predicting participation, early onset and later persistence in officially recorded offending. *Criminal Behavior and Mental Health*, **1**, 1–33.

Flannery, D. J., Vaszony, A. T., Torquati, J., & Fridrich, A. (1994). Ethnic and gender differences in risk for early adolescent substance use. *Journal of Youth and Adolescence*, **23**, 195–213.

Fleming, J. P., Kellam, S. G., & Brown, C. H. (1982). Early predictors of age at first use of alcohol, marijuana and cigarettes. *Drug and Alcohol Dependence*, **9**, 285–303.

Fletcher, A. C., Darling, N., & Steinberg, L. (1995). Parental monitoring and peer influences on adolescent substance use. In J. McCord (Ed.), *Coercion and punishment in long term perspectives* (pp. 259–271). New York: Cambridge University Press.

Fletcher, A. C., Steinberg, L., & Williams-Wheeler, M. (2004). Parental influences on adolescent problem behavior: Revisiting Stattin and Kerr. *Child Development*, **75**, 781–796.

Fontaine, R. G., Yang, C., Dodge, K. A., Bates, J. E., & Pettit, G. S. (2008). Testing an individual systems model of Response Evaluation and Decision (RED) and antisocial behavior across adolescence. *Child Development*, **79**(2), 462–475.

Gatti, U., Tremblay, R. E., Vitaro, F., & McDuff, P. (2005). Youth gangs, delinquency and drug use: A test of selection, facilitation, and enhancement hypotheses. *Journal of Child Psychology and Psychiatry*, **46**(11), 1178–1190.

Gershoff, E. T. (2002). Parental corporal punishment and associated child behaviors and experiences: A meta-analytic and theoretical review. *Psychological Bulletin*, **128**, 539–579.

Gifford-Smith, M., Dodge, K. A., Dishion, T. J., & McCord, J. (2005). Peer influence in children and adolescents: Crossing the bridge between developmental and intervention sciences. *Journal of Abnormal Child Psychology*, **33**, 255–265.

Glantz, M. D. (2002). Introduction to the special edition on the impact of childhood psychopathology interventions on subsequent substance abuse: Pieces of the puzzle. *Journal of Consulting and Clinical Psychology*, **70**, 1203–1206.

Glantz, M. D., & Leshner, A. I. (2000). Drug abuse and developmental psychopathology. *Development and Psychopathology*, **12**, 795–814.

Goodnight, J. A., Bates, J. E., Newman, J. P., Dodge, K. A., & Pettit, G. S. (2006). The interactive influences of friend deviance and reward dominance on the development of externalizing behavior during middle adolescence. *Journal of Abnormal Child Psychology*, **34**, 573–583.

Goodnight, J. A., Bates, J. E., Pettit, G. S., & Dodge, K. A. (2008). Parents' campaigns to reduce their children's conduct problems: Interactions with temperamental resistance to control. *European Journal of Developmental Science*, **2**(1/2), 100–119.

Goodwin, D. W. (1985). Alcoholism and genetics: The sins of the fathers. *Archives of General Psychiatry*, **42**, 171–174.

Gottfredson, D. C. (1988). *Issues in adolescent drug use*. Unpublished final report to the U.S. Department of Justice, Johns Hopkins University, Center for Research on Elementary and Middle Schools, Baltimore, MD.

Gottfredson, D., Kearley, B., & Bushway, S. (2008). Substance use, drug treatment, and crime: An examination of intra-individual variation in a drug-court population. *Journal of Drug Issues*, **38**(2), 601–630.

Gottfredson, D. C., & Koper, C. S. (1996). Race and sex differences in the prediction of drug use. *Journal of Consulting and Clinical Psychology*, **64**, 305–313.

Gottlieb, G. (1997). *Synthesizing nature-nurture: Prenatal roots of instinctive behavior.* Mahwah, NJ: Erlbaum.

Granic, I., & Patterson, G. R. (2006). Toward a comprehensive model of antisocial development: A dynamic systems approach. *Psychological Review*, **113**, 101–131.

Gray, J. A. (1987). *The psychology of fear and stress* (2nd ed.). New York: McGraw Hill.

Greenberg, M. L., Lengua, L. S., Coie, J., Pinderhughes, E. E., & the Conduct Problems Prevention Research Group. (1999). Predicting developmental outcomes at school entry using a multiple-risk model: Four American communities. *Developmental Psychology*, **35**, 403–417.

Greene, R. W., Biederman, J., Faraone, S. V., Sienna, M., & Garcia-Jetton, J. (1997). Adolescent outcome of boys with attention deficit/hyperactivity disorder and social disability: Results from a 4-year longitudinal follow-up study. *Journal of Consulting and Clinical Psychology*, **65**, 758–767.

Greene, R. W., Biederman, J., Faraone, S. V., Wilens, T. E., Mick, E., & Blier, H. K. (1999). Further validation of social impairment as a predictor of substance use disorders: Findings from a sample of siblings of boys with and without ADHD. *Journal of Consulting and Clinical Psychology*, **62**, 410–414.

Grimes, C. L., Klein, T. P., & Putallaz, M. (2004). Parents' relationships with their parents and peers: Influences on children's social development. [References]. In J. B. Kupersmidt & K. A. Dodge (Eds.), *Children's peer relations: From development to intervention: Decade of behavior* (pp. 141–158). Washington, DC: American Psychological Association.

Griffin, K. W., Botvin, G. J., Epstein, J. A., Doyle, M. M., & Diaz, T. (2000). Psychosocial and behavioral factors in early adolescence as predictors of heavy drinking among high school seniors. *Journal of Studies on Alcohol*, **61**, 603.

Gruber, E., DiClemente, R. J., Anderson, M., & Lodico, M. (1996). Early drinking onset and its association with alcohol use and problem behavior in late adolescence. *Preventive Medicine: An International Journal Devoted to Practice and Theory*, **25**, 293–300.

Hansell, N. K., Agrawal, A., Whitfield, J. B., Morley, K. I., Zhu, G., Lind, P. A., et al. (2008). Long-term stability and heritability of telephone interview measures of alcohol consumption and dependence. *Twin Research and Human Genetics*, **11**, 287–305.

Hansen, W. B., Graham, J. W., Sobel, J. L., Shelton, D. R., Flay, B. R., & Johnson, C. A. (1987). The consistency of peer and parent influences on tobacco, alcohol, and marijuana use among young adolescents. *Journal of Behavioral Medicine*, **10**, 559–579.

Harrist, A. W., Zaia, A. F., Bates, J. E., Dodge, K. A., & Pettit, G. S. (1997). Subtypes of social withdrawal in early childhood: Sociometric status and social-cognitive differences across four years. *Child Development*, **68**, 332–348.

Hawkins, J. D., Catalano, R. F., & Miller, J. Y. (1992). Risk and protective factors for alcohol and other drug problems in adolescence and early adulthood. *Psychological Bulletin*, **112**, 64–105.

Hawkins, J. D., Graham, J. W., Maguin, E., Abbott, R., Hill, K. G., & Catalano, R. F. (1997). Exploring the effects of age of alcohol use initiation and psychosocial risk factors on subsequent alcohol misuse. *Journal of Studies on Alcohol*, **58**, 280–290.

Heckman, J. J., & Masterov, D. V. (2006). *The productivity argument for investing in young children.* Working Paper No. 5, Committee for Economic Development, Invest in Kids Working Group.

Hollingshead, A. A. (1979). *Four-Factor Index of Social Status.* Unpublished manuscript, Yale University, New Haven, CT.

Hops, H., Tildesley, E., Lichenstein, E., Ary, D., & Sherman, L. (1990). Parent–adolescent problem solving interactions and drug use. *American Journal of Drug and Alcohol Abuse*, **16**, 239–258.

Hoyle, R. H. (2000). Personality processes and problem behavior. *Journal of Personality*, **68**, 953–966.

Horowitz, F. D. (1987). *Exploring developmental theories: Toward a structural/behavioral model of development*. Mahwah, NJ: Lawrence Erlbaum.

Hrubec, Z., & Omenn, G. S. (1981). Evidence of genetic predisposition to alcoholic cirrhosis and psychosis: Twin concordances for alcoholism and its biological end points by zygosity among male veterans. *Alcoholism*, **5**, 207–215.

Hundleby, J. D., & Mercer, G. W. (1987). Family and friends as social environments and their relationship to young adolescents' use of alcohol, tobacco, and marijuana. *Journal of Clinical Psychology*, **44**, 125–134.

Institute of Medicine. (1994). *Reducing risks for mental disorders: Frontiers for preventive intervention research*. Washington, DC: National Academy Press.

Isaacs, J. B. (2007). *Cost-effective investments in children. Budget Options Series*. Washington, DC: Brookings Institution.

Jackson, C., Hendrikson, L., Dickinson, D., & Levine, D. W. (1997). The early use of alcohol and tobacco: Its relation to children's competence and parents' behavior. *American Journal of Public Health*, **87**, 359–364.

Jessor, R., Donovan, J. E., & Windmer, K. (1980). *Psychosocial factors in adolescent alcohol and drug use: The 1980 National Sample Study and the 1974–78 Panel Study*. Unpublished final report, University of Colorado, Institute of Behavioral Science, Boulder.

Jessor, R., & Jessor, S. (1977). *Problem behavior and psychosocial development: A Longitudinal Study of Youth*. San Diego, CA: Academic Press.

Johnson, C. A., Schoutz, F. C., & Locke, T. P. (1984). Relationships between adolescent drug use and parental drug behaviors. *Adolescence*, **19**, 295–299.

Johnston, L. D., O'Malley, P. M., & Bachman, J. G. (1985). *Use of licit and illicit drugs by America's high school students, 1975–1984*. Rockville, MD: National Institute of Drug Abuse.

Johnston, L. D., O'Malley, P. M., & Bachman, J. G. (1995). *National survey results on drug use from the Monitoring the Future Study, 1975–1994. Vol. 1: Secondary school students*. Rockville, MD: National Institute on Drug Abuse.

Johnston, L. D., O'Malley, P. M., & Bachman, J. G. (1999). *National survey results on drug use from the Monitoring the Future Study, 1975–1998. Vol. I: Secondary school students* (NIH Publication No. 99-4660). Bethesda, MD: National Institute on Drug Abuse.

Johnston, L. D., O'Malley, P. M., & Bachman, J. G. (2002). *National survey results on drug use from the Monitoring the Future Study. 2001*. Rockville, MD: National Institute on Drug Abuse.

Johnston, L. D., O'Malley, P. M., Bachman, J. G., & Schulenberg, J. E. (2008). *Monitoring the Future national results on adolescent drug use: Overview of key findings 2007* (NIH Publication No. 08-6418). Bethesda, MD: National Institute on Drug Abuse.

Kandel, D. B. (1978). Homophily, selection, and socialization in adolescent friendships. *American Journal of Sociology*, **84**, 427–436.

Kandel, D. B., & Andrews, K. (1987). Processes of adolescent socialization by parents and peers. *International Journal of Addictions*, **22**, 319–342.

Kandel, D., & Davies, M. (1992). Progression to regular marijuana involvement: Phenomenology and risk factors for near-daily use. In M. Glantz & R. Pickens (Eds.), *Vulnerability to drug abuse* (pp. 211–253). Washington, DC: American Psychological Association.

Kandel, D. B., Davies, M., Karus, D., & Yamaguchi, K. (1986). The consequences in young adulthood of adolescent drug involvement. *Archives of General Psychiatry*, **43**, 746–754.

Kandel, D. B., Johnson, J. G., Bird, H. R., Weissman, M. M., Goodman, S. H., Lahey, B. B., et al. (1999). Psychiatric comorbidity among adolescents with substance use disorders:

Findings from the MECA study. *Journal of the American Academy of Child and Adolescent Psychiatry*, **38**, 693–699.

Kandel, D. B., & Logan, J. A. (1984). Patterns of drug use from adolescence to young adulthood: I. Periods of risk for initiation, continued use, and discontinuation. *American Journal of Public Health*, **74**, 660–666.

Kandel, D. B., & Yamaguchi, K. (1985). Developmental patterns of the use of legal, illegal, and medically prescribed psychotropic drugs from adolescence to young adulthood. In C. L. Jones & R. J. Battjes (Eds.), *Etiology of drug abuse: Implications for prevention* (NIDA research monograph 56) (pp. 193–235). Rockville, MD: National Institute on Drug Abuse.

Kandel, D., Yamaguchi, K., & Chen, K. (1992). Stages of drug involvement from adolescence to adulthood: Further evidence for the gateway theory. *Journal of Studies on Alcohol*, **53**, 447–457.

Kandel, D. B., Johnson, J. G., Bird, H. R., Canino, G., Goodman, S. H., Lahey, B. B., et al. (1997). Psychiatric disorders associated with substance use among children and adolescents: Findings from the Methods for the Epidemiology of Child and Adolescent Mental Disorders (MECA) Study. *Journal of Abnormal Child Psychology*, **25**, 121–132.

Kaplan, S. J., Pelcovitz, D., Salzinger, S., Weiner, M., Mandel, F. S., Lesser, M. L., et al. (1998). Adolescent physical abuse: Risk for adolescent psychiatric disorders. *American Journal of Psychiatry*, **155**, 954–959.

Kaplow, J. B., Curran, P. J., Angold, A., & Costello, E. J. (2001). The prospective relation between dimensions of anxiety and the initiation of adolescent alcohol use. *Journal of Clinical Child Psychology*, **30**, 316–326.

Kaplow, J. B., Curran, P. J., Dodge, K. A., & the Conduct Problems Prevention Research Group. (2002). Child, parent, and peer predictors of early-onset substance use: A multisite longitudinal study. *Journal of Abnormal Child Psychology*, **30**, 199–216.

Kellam, S. G., Ensminger, M. E., & Simon, M. B. (1980). Mental health in first grade and teenage drug, alcohol, and cigarette use. *Drug and Alcohol Dependence*, **5**, 273–304.

Kelly, D. H., & Balch, R. W. (1971). Social origins and school failure: A reexamination of Cohen's theory of working-class delinquency. *Pacific Social Review*, **14**, 413–430.

Kendall, P. C., & Kessler, R. C. (2002). The impact of childhood psychopathology interventions on subsequent substance abuse: Policy implications, comments, and recommendations. *Journal of Consulting and Clinical Psychology*, **70**, 1303–1306.

Kendler, K. S., Bulik, C. M., Silberg, J., Hettema, J. M., Myers, J., & Prescott, C. A. (2000). Childhood sexual abuse and adult psychiatric and substance use disorders in women: An epidemiological and cotwin control analysis. *Archives of General Psychiatry*, **57**, 953–959.

Kerns, K. A. (1998). Individual differences in friendship quality: Links to child–mother attachment. In W. M. Bukowski, A. F. Newcomb, & W. W. Hartup (Eds.), *The company they keep* (pp. 137–157). New York: Cambridge University Press.

Kerr, M., & Stattin, H. (2000). What parents know, how they know it, and several forms of adolescent adjustment: Further support for a reinterpretation of monitoring. *Developmental Psychology*, **36**, 366–380.

Kessler, R. C., Aguilar-Gaxiola, S., Andrade, L., Bijl, R., Borges, G., Carveo-Anduaga, J. J., et al. (2001). Mental-substance comorbidities in the ICPE surveys. *Psychiatria Fennica*, **32**, 62–80.

Kilpatrick, D. G., Acierno, R., Saunders, B., Resnick, H. S., Best, C. L., & Schnurr, P. P. (2000). Risk factors for adolescent substance abuse and dependence: Data from a national sample. *Journal of Consulting and Clinical Psychology*, **68**, 19–30.

Koot, H. M., & Timmermans, M. (2007). *Developmental cascades between internalizing and externalizing problems, psychiatric disorder, and social functioning*. Paper presented at the Biennial Meeting of the Society for Research in Child Development, Boston.

Kosterman, R., Hawkins, J. D., Guo, J., Catalano, R. F., & Abbott, R. D. (2000). The dynamics of alcohol and marijuana initiation: Patterns and predictors of first use in adolescence. *American Journal of Public Health*, **90**, 360–366.

Kraemer, H. C. (2008). Toward non-parametric and clinically meaningful moderators and mediators. *Statistics in Medicine*, **27**, 1679–1692.

Krohn, M. D., & Thornberry, T. P. (1993). Network theory: A model for understanding drug abuse among African-American and Hispanic youth. In M. R. De La Rosa & J. R. Adrados (Eds.), *Drug abuse among minority youth: Advances in research and methodology* (pp. 102–127). Rockville, MD: National Institute on Drug Abuse.

Kupersmidt, J. B., Coie, J. D., & Dodge, K. A. (1990). The role of poor peer relationships in the development of disorder. In S. R. Asher & J. D. Coie (Eds.), *Peer rejection in childhood* (pp. 274–305). New York: Cambridge University Press.

Laird, R. D., Jordan, K., Dodge, K. A., Pettit, G. S., & Bates, J. E. (2001). Peer rejection in childhood, involvement with antisocial peers in early adolescence, and the development of externalizing problems. *Development and Psychopathology*, **13**, 337–354.

Laird, R. D., Pettit, G. S., Dodge, K. A., & Bates, J. E. (2003). Change in parents' monitoring knowledge: Links with parenting, relationship quality, adolescent beliefs, and antisocial behavior. *Social Development*, **12**, 401–419.

Laird, R. D., Pettit, G. S., Dodge, K. A., & Bates, J. E. (1999). Best friendships, group relationships, and antisocial behavior in early adolescence. *Journal of Early Adolescence*, **19**, 413–437.

Laird, R. D., Pettit, G. S., Dodge, K. A., & Bates, J. E. (2005). Peer relationship antecedents of delinquent behavior in late adolescence: Is there evidence of demographic group differences in developmental processes? *Development and Psychopathology*, **17**, 1–18.

Landrine, H., Richardson, J., Klonoff, E., & Flay, B. (1994). Cultural diversity in the predictors for adolescent cigarette smoking: The relative influence of peers. *Journal of Behavioral Medicine*, **17**, 331–346.

Lerner, J., & Vicary, J. (1984). Difficult temperament and drug use: Analysis from the New York longitudinal study. *Journal of Drug Education*, **14**, 1–8.

Lerner, R. M., & Castellino, D. R. (2002). Contemporary developmental theory and adolescence: Developmental systems and applied developmental science. *Journal of Adolescent Health*, **31**, 122–135.

Levin, E. D., Rezvani, A. H., Montoya, D., Rose, J. E., & Swartzwelder, H. S. (2003). Adolescent-onset nicotine self-administration modeled in female rats. *Psychopharmacology*, **169**, 141–149.

Lewinsohn, P. M., Rohde, P., & Seeley, J. R. (1995). Adolescent psychopathology: III. The clinical consequences of comorbidity. *Journal of the American Academy of Child and Adolescent Psychiatry*, **34**, 510–519.

Lewis, C. E., Robins, L. N., & Rice, J. (1985). Association of alcoholism with antisocial personality in urban men. *Journal of Nervous and Mental Disease*, **173**, 166–174.

Little , M., Weaver , S. R., King , K. M., Liu , F., & Chassin , L. (2008). Historical change in the link between adolescent deviance proneness and marijuana use, 1979–2004. *Prevention Science*, **9**, 4–16.

Little, P. J., Kuhn, C. M., Wilson, W. A., & Swartzwelder, H. S. (1996). Differential effects of ethanol in adolescent and adult rats. *Alcoholism: Clinical and Experimental Research*, **20**, 1346–1351.

Liu, X., & Kaplan, H. B. (1996). Gender-related differences in circumstances surrounding initiation and escalation of alcohol and other substance use/abuse. *Deviant Behavior*, **17**, 71–106.

Lochner, L. J., & Moretti, E. (2004). The effect of education on crime: Evidence from prison inmates, arrests and self-reports. *American Economic Review*, 155–189.

Loeber, R., Stouthamer-Loeber, M., & White, H. R. (1999). Developmental aspects of delinquency and internalizing problems and their association with persistent juvenile substance use between ages 7 and 18. *Journal of Clinical Child Psychology*, **28**, 322–332.

Lukas, S. E., & Wetherington, C. L. (2005). Sex- and gender-related differences in the neurobiology of drug abuse. *Clinical Neuroscience Research*, **5**, 75–87.

MacKinnon, D. P., Lockwood, C. M., Hoffman, J. M., West, S. G., & Sheets, V. (2002a). A comparison of methods to test mediation and other intervening variable effects. *Psychological Methods*, **7**, 83–104.

MacKinnon, D. P., Lockwood, C. M., Hoffman, J. M., West, S. G., & Sheets, V. (2002b). Tables referenced in MacKinnon, D.P., Lockwood, C.M., Hoffman, J.M., West, S.G., & Sheets, V. (in press, 2002). A comparison of methods to test mediation and other intervening variable effects. *Psychological Methods*. Retrieved January 17, 2009, from http://www.public.asu.edu/~davidpm/ripl/freqdist.pdf

Maddahian, E., Newcomb, M. D., & Bentler, P. M. (1988). Adolescent drug use and intention to use drugs: Concurrent and longitudinal analyses of four ethnic groups. *Addictive Behaviors*, **13**, 191–195.

Mannuza, S., Klein, R. G., Bessler, A., Malloy, P., & LaPadula, M. (1998). Adult psychiatric status of hyperactive boys grown up. *American Journal of Psychiatry*, **155**, 493–498.

Masse, L. C., & Tremblay, R. E. (1997). Behavior of boys in kindergarten and the onset of substance use during adolescence. *Archives of General Psychiatry*, **54**, 62–68.

Masten, A. S., Faden, V. B., Zucker, R. A., & Spear, L. P. (2008). Underage drinking: A developmental framework. *Pediatrics*, **121**(Suppl. 4), S235–S251.

Masten, A. S., Roisman, G. I., Long, J. D., Burt, K. B., Obradović, J., Riley, J. R., et al. (2005). Developmental cascades: Linking academic achievement, externalizing and internalizing symptoms over 20 years. *Developmental Psychology*, **41**, 733–746.

McCarthy, W. J., & Anglin, M. D. (1990). Narcotics addicts: Effect of family and parental risk factors on timing of emancipation, drug use onset, pre-addiction incarcerations and educational achievement. *Journal of Drug Issues*, **20**, 99–123.

McCord, J. (1991). Questioning the value of punishment. *Social Problems*, **38**, 167–179.

McFadyen-Ketchum, S. A., Bates, J. E., Dodge, K. A., & Pettit, G. S. (1996). Patterns of change in early child aggressive–disruptive behavior: Gender differences in predictors from early coercive and affectionate mother–child interactions. *Child Development*, **67**, 2417–2433.

McLoyd, V. C. (1990). The impact of economic hardship on Black families and children: Psychological distress, parenting, and socioemotional development. *Child Development*, **61**, 311–346.

McMahon, R. J., Collins, L., & Conduct Problems Prevention Research Group. (2000). *Relationship of pre-existing psychopathology to early tobacco use by school-age youth*. Paper presented at the 2000 meeting of the Society for Research in Adolescence, Chicago.

Merikangas, J., Stolar, M., Stevens, D., Goulet, J., Preisig, M., Fenton, B., et al. (1998). Familial transmission of substance use disorders. *Archives of General Psychiatry*, **55**, 973–979.

Miller, T. L. (2004). The social costs of adolescent problem behavior. In A. Biglan, P. A. Brennan, S. L. Foster, H. D. Holder, T. L. Miller & P. B. Cunningham (Eds.), *Helping adolescents at risk: Preventions of multiple problem behaviors*. New York: Guilford Press.

Miron, J. A. (December, 2008). *The budgetary implications of drug prohibition*. Working paper. Retrieved from http://leap.cc/dia/miron-economic-report.pdf

Modzeleski, W. (2006). *Prevention of substance use in public schools*. Presentation made to Duke University, Durham, NC.

Moffitt, T. E. (1993). Adolescence-limited and life-course-persistent antisocial behavior: A developmental taxonomy. *Psychological Review*, **100**, 674–701.

Moilanen, K. L., & Shaw, D. S. (2007). *Developmental cascades: Externalizing, internalizing and academic competence from middle childhood to early adolescence.* Paper presented at the Biennial Meeting of the Society for Research in Child Development, Boston.

Murray, D. M., & Stabenau, J. R. (1982). Genetic factors in alcoholism predisposition. In M. Pattison (Ed.), *Encyclopedic handbook of alcoholism* (pp. 135–144). New York: Gardner Press.

Muthén, L. K., & Muthén, B. O. (2002). *Mplus version 2.1: Addendum to the Mplus User's Guide.* Retrieved July 10, 2002, from http://www.statmodel.com/version2.html

National Center on Addiction and Substance Abuse. (2003). *The formative years: Pathways to substance abuse among girls and young women ages 8–22.* New York: Columbia University.

National Institute on Drug Abuse. (2002). *2002 Monitoring the Future Survey shows decrease in use of marijuana, club drugs, cigarettes and tobacco.* Retrieved September 8, 2003, from http://www.nida.nih.gov/Newsroom/02/NR12-16.html

National Research Council. (2004). *Reducing underage drinking: A collective responsibility.* Washington, DC: National Academies Press.

Needle, R., Su, S., & Lavee, Y. (1989). A comparison of the empirical utility of three composite measures of adolescent drug involvement. *Addictive Behaviors*, **14**, 429–441.

Nestler, E. J., & Landsman, D. (2001). Learning about addiction from the genome. *Nature*, **409**, 834–835.

Newcomb, M. D., & Bentler, P. M. (1988). Impact of adolescent drug use and social support on problems of young adults. *Journal of Abnormal Psychology*, **97**, 64–75.

Newcomb, M. D., & Felix-Ortiz, M. (1992). Multiple protective and risk factors for drug use and abuse: Cross-sectional and prospective findings. *Journal of Personality and Social Psychology*, **63**, 280–296.

Obradovic, J., & Masten, A. S. (2007). *Linking academic achievement, social competence and internalizing symptoms over 20 years: Testing developmental cascade models.* Paper presented at the Biennial Meeting of the Society for Research in Child Development, Boston.

Office of National Drug Control Policy. (1999). *The 1999 national drug control strategy.* Washington, DC: Author.

Panksepp, J. (1998). *Affective neuroscience—The foundations of human and animal emotions.* Oxford: Oxford University Press.

Parke, R. D., Burks, V., Carson, J., Neville, B., & Boyum, L. (1994). Family–peer relationships: A tripartite model. In R. D. Parke & S. Kellam (Eds.), *Family relationships with other social systems* (pp. 86–112). Hillsdale, NJ: Lawrence Erlbaum.

Patterson, G. R. (1986). Performance models for antisocial boys. *American Psychologist*, **41**, 432–444.

Patterson, G. R., Capaldi, D. M., & Bank, L. (1991). An early starter model predicting delinquency. In D. J. Pepler & K. A. Ruben (Eds.), *The development and treatment of childhood aggression* (pp. 139–168). Hillsdale, NJ: Lawrence Erlbaum.

Patterson, G. R., Reid, J. B., & Dishion, T. J. (1992). *A social learning approach: Vol. 4, Antisocial boys.* Eugene, OR: Castalia Press.

Penning, M., & Barnes, G. E. (1982). Adolescent marijuana use: A review. *International Journal of Addictions*, **17**, 749–791.

Petraitis, J., Flay, B. R., & Miller, T. Q. (1995). Reviewing theories of adolescent substance use: Organizing pieces in the puzzle. *Psychological Bulletin*, **117**, 67–86.

Pettit, G. S., Bates, J. E., & Dodge, K. A. (1997). Supportive parenting, ecological context, and children's adjustment: A seven-year longitudinal study. *Child Development*, **68**, 908–923.

Pettit, G. S., Bates, J. E., Dodge, K. A., & Meece, D. W. (1999). The impact of after-school peer contact on early adolescent externalizing problems is moderated by parental monitoring, neighborhood safety, and prior adjustment. *Child Development*, **70**, 768–778.

Pettit, G. S., Keiley, M. K., Laird, R. D., Bates, J. E., & Dodge, K. A. (2007). Predicting the developmental course of mother-reported monitoring across childhood and adolescence from early proactive parenting, child temperament, and parents' worries. *Journal of Family Psychology*, **21**, 206–217.

Pomerleau, C. S., Pomerleau, O. F., Flessland, K. A., & Basson, S. M. (1992). Relationship of TPQ scores to smoking variables in female and male smokers. *Journal of Substance Abuse*, **4**, 143–153.

Posner, J. K., & Vandell, D. L. (1994). Low-income children's after-school care: Are there beneficial effects of after-school programs? *Child Development*, **65**, 440–456.

Prinstein, M. J., & LaGreca, A. M. (1999). Links between mothers' and children's social competence and associations with maternal adjustment. *Journal of Clinical Child Psychology*, **28**, 197–210.

Putallaz, M., Klein, T. P., Costanzo, P. R., & Hedges, L. A. (1994). Relating mothers' social framing to their children's entry competence with peers. *Social Development*, **3**, 222–237.

Reid, J. B., Patterson, G. R. & Snyder, J. (Eds.). (2000). *Antisocial behavior in children and adolescents: A developmental analysis and model for intervention*. Washington, DC: American Psychological Association.

Reinherz, H. Z., Giaconia, R. M., Hauf, A. M., Wasserman, M. S., & Paradis, A. D. (2000). General and specific childhood risk factors for depression and drug disorders by early adulthood. *Journal of the American Academy of Child and Adolescent Psychiatry*, **39**, 223–231.

Robins, L. N., & Przybeck, T. R. (1985). Age of onset of drug use as a factor in drug and other disorders. In C. L. Jones & R. J. Battjes (Eds.), *Etiology of drug abuse: Implications for prevention* (pp. 178–192). Washington, DC: National Institute on Drug Abuse.

Robins, L. N., & Ratcliff, K. S. (1979). Continuation of antisocial behavior into adulthood. *International Journal of Mental Health*, **7**, 96–116.

Rowe, D. C., Vazsonyi, A. T., & Flannery, D. J. (1994). No more than skin deep: Ethnic and racial similarity in developmental process. *Psychological Review*, **101**, 396–413.

Rubin, D. B. (1987). *Multiple imputation for nonresponse in surveys*. New York: John Wiley and Sons.

Rubin, K. H., Bukowski, W. M. & Laursen, B. (Eds.) (2008). *Handbook of peer interactions, relationships, and groups*. New York: Guilford Press.

Rutter, M., & Garmezy, N. (1983). Developmental psychopathology. In P. H. Mussen & E. M. Hetherington (Eds.), *Handbook of child psychology: Vol. 4. Socialization, personality and social development* (pp. 775–911). New York: Wiley.

Sameroff, A. J. (2000). Developmental systems and psychopathology. *Development and Psychopathology*, **12**, 297–312.

Sameroff, A. J. (Ed.). (2009). *Transactional development: Operationalizing a dynamic system*. Washington, DC: American Psychological Association.

Sameroff, A. J., & Chandler, M. J. (1975). Reproductive risk and the continuum of caretaking casualty. In F. D. Horowitz, M. Hetherington, S. Scarr-Salapatek & G. Siegal (Eds.), *Review of child development research* (Vol. 4, pp. 187–244). Chicago: University of Chicago Press.

Sameroff, A. J., & MacKenzie, M. J. (2003). Research strategies for capturing transactional models of development: The limits of the possible. *Development and Psychopathology*, **15**, 613–640.

Sampson, R. J., & Laub, J. H. (1994). Urban poverty and the family context of delinquency: A new look at structure and process in a classic study. *Child Development*, **65**, 523–540.

SAS Institute. (2003). *SAS 8.2* [Computer software]. Cary, NC: Author.

Schafer, J. L. (1999). Multiple imputation: A primer. *Statistical Methods in Medical Research*, **8**, 3–15.

Selzer, M. L., Vinokur, A., & Van Rooijen, C. (1975). A self-administered Short Michigan Alcoholism Screening test (SMAST). *Journal of Studies on Alcohol*, **36**, 117–126.

Shedler, J., & Block, J. (1990). Adolescent drug use and psychological health: A longitudinal inquiry. *American Psychologist*, **45**, 612–630.

Shoal, G. D., & Giancola, P. R. (2003). Negative affectivity and drug use in adolescent boys: Moderating and mediating mechanisms. *Journal of Personality and Social Psychology*, **84**, 221–233.

Shonkoff, P. & Phillips, D. A. (Eds.). (2000). *From neurons to neighborhoods: The science of early childhood development*. Washington, DC: National Academy Press.

Siebenbruner, J., Englund, M. M., Egeland, B., & Hudson, K. (2006). Developmental antecedents of late adolescence substance use patterns. *Development and Psychopathology*, **189**(2), 551–571.

Simcha-Fagan, O., Gersten, J. C., & Langner, T. (1986). Early precursors and concurrent correlates of illicit drug use in adolescents. *Journal of Drug Issues*, **16**, 7–28.

Simons, R. L., Conger, R. D., & Whitbeck, L. B. (1988). A multistage social learning model of the influences of family and peers upon adolescent substance abuse. *Journal of Drug Issues*, **24**, 9–24.

Snyder, J., Reid, J., & Patterson, G. (2003). A social learning model of child and adolescent antisocial behavior. In B. B. Lahey, T. E. Moffitt & A. Caspi (Eds.), *Causes of conduct disorder and juvenile delinquency* (pp. 27–48). New York: Guilford.

Stattin, H., & Kerr, M. (2000). Parental monitoring: A reinterpretation. *Child Development*, **71**, 1072–1085.

Steinberg, L., Dahl, R., Keating, D., Kupfer, D., Masten, A., & Pine, D. (2006). Psychopathology in adolescence: Integrating affective neuroscience with the study of context. In D. Cicchetti & D. Cohen (Eds.), *Developmental psychopathology, Vol. 2: Developmental neuroscience* (pp. 710–741). New York: Wiley.

Stice, E., & Barrera, M. (1995). A longitudinal examination of the reciprocal relations between perceived parenting and adolescents' substance use and externalizing behaviors. *Developmental Psychology*, **31**, 322–334.

Straus, M. A., & Stewart, J. H. (1999). Corporal punishment by American parents: National data on prevalence, chronicity, severity, and duration, in relation to child and family characteristics. *Clinical Child and Family Psychology Review*, **2**, 55–70.

Substance Abuse and Mental Health Services Administration. (1997). *Preliminary results from the 1996 National Household Survey on Drug Abuse*. Retrieved from http://www.oas.samhsa.gov/nhsda/PE1996/HTTOC.HTM

Substance Abuse and Mental Health Services Administration. (2005). *National expenditures for mental health services and substance abuse treatment, 1991–2001* (DHHS Publication No. SMA 05-3999). Rockville, MD: Author.

Substance Abuse and Mental Health Services Administration, Office of Applied Statistics. (2009). *The NSDUH Report: Treatment for substance use and depression among adults, by race/ethnicity*. Rockville, MD: Author.

Substance Abuse and Mental Health Services Administration, Office of Applied Statistics. (2009). *The NSDUH Report: Young adults' need for and receipt of alcohol and illicit drug use treatment: 2007*. Rockville, MD: Author.

Tabakoff, B., & Hoffman, P. L. (1988). Genetics and biological markers of risk for alcoholism. *Public Health Reports*, **103**, 690–698.

Tangney, J. P., Hill-Barlow, D., Wagner, P. E., Marschall, D. E., Borenstein, J. K., Sanftner, J., et al. (1996). Assessing individual differences in constructive versus destructive responses to anger across the lifespan. *Journal of Personality and Social Psychology*, **70**, 780–796.

Tarter, R. E., & Vanyukov, M. (1994). Alcoholism: A developmental disorder. *Journal of Consulting and Clinical Psychology*, **62**, 1096–1107.

Tarter, R. E., Vanyukov, M., Giancola, P. R., Dawes, M. A., Blackson, T., Mezzich, A. C., et al. (1999). Etiology of early age onset substance use disorder: A maturational perspective. *Developmental Psychopathology*, **11**, 657–683.

Teitelbaum, L. M., & Carey, K. B. (2000). Temporal stability of alcohol screening measures in a psychiatric setting. *Psychology of Addictive Behaviors*, **14**, 401–404.

Thelan, E., Ulrich, B. D., & Wolff, P. H. (1991). Hidden skills: A dynamic systems analysis of treadmill stepping during the first year. *Monographs of the Society for Research in Child Development*), **56**(1).

Thomas, B. S. (1996). A path analysis of gender differences in adolescent onset of alcohol, tobacco and other drug use (ATOD), reported ATOD use and adverse consequences of ATOD use. *Journal of Addictive Diseases*, **15**, 33–52.

Thornberry, T. P., Krohn, M. D., Lizotte, A. J., & Chard-Wierschem, D. (1993). The role of juvenile gangs in facilitating delinquent behavior. *Journal of Research in Crime and Delinquency*, **30**, 55–87.

Tolan, P. H., & Dodge, K. A. (2005). Children's mental health as a primary care and concern: A system for comprehensive support and service. *American Psychologist*, **60**(6), 601–614.

Uniform Crime Report. (June 1, 2009). *Crime in the United States: Preliminary annual uniform crime report*. Washington, DC: U.S. Department of Justice, Bureau of Justice Statistics. Retrieved from http://www.fbi.gov/ucr/08prelim

U.S. Department of Health and Human Services. (1994). *Preventing tobacco use among young people: A report of the surgeon general*. Atlanta, GA: U.S. Department of Health and Human Services, Public Health Service, Centers for Disease Control and Prevention, National Center for Chronic Disease Prevention and Health Promotion, Office on Smoking and Health.

Van Kammen, W. B., & Loeber, R. (1994). Are fluctuations in delinquent activities related to the onset and offset in juvenile illegal drug use and drug dealing? *The Journal of Drug Issues*, **24**, 9–24.

Waddington, C. H. (1962). *New patterns in genetics and development*. New York: Columbia University Press.

Weinberg, N. Z., Rahdert, E., Colliver, J. D., & Glantz, M. D. (1998). Adolescent substance abuse: A review of the past 10 years. *Journal of the American Academy of Child and Adolescent Psychiatry*, **37**, 252–261.

Weinberg, N. Z., & Glantz, M. D. (1999). Child psychopathology risk factors for drug abuse: Overview. *Journal of Clinical Child Psychology*, **28**, 290–297.

Widom, C. S., Ireland, T., & Glynn, P. J. (1995). Alcohol abuse in abused and neglected children followed-up: Are they at increased risk? *Journal of Studies on Alcohol*, **56**, 207–217.

Willett, J. B., & Singer, J. D. (1993). Investigating onset, cessation, relapse, and recovery: Why you should, and how you can, use discrete-time survival analysis to examine event occurrence. *Journal of Consulting and Clinical Psychology*, **61**, 952–965.

Wills, T. A., DuHammel, K., & Vaccaro, D. (1995). Activity and mood temperament as predictors of adolescent substance use. *Journal of Personality and Social Psychology*, **68**, 901–916.

Wills, T. A., Sandy, J. M., Yaeger, A., & Shinar, O. (2001). Family risk factors and adolescent substance use: Moderation effects for temperament dimensions. *Developmental Psychology*, **37**, 283–297.

Wills, T. A., Vaccaro, D., & McNamara, G. (1994). Novelty seeking, risk taking, and related constructs as predictors of adolescent substance use: An application of Cloninger's theory. *Journal of Substance Abuse*, **6**, 1–20.

Wills, T. A., & Yaeger, A. M. (2003). Family factors and adolescent substance use: Models and mechanisms. *Current Directions in Psychological Science*, **12**, 222–226.

Windle, M. (1991). The difficult temperament in adolescence: Associations with substance use, family support, and problem behaviors. *Journal of Clinical Psychology*, **47**, 310–315.

Windle, M. (2000). Parental, sibling, and peer influences on adolescent substance use and alcohol problems. *Applied Developmental Psychology*, **4**, 98–110.

Windle, M., & Lerner, R. M. (1986). The Revised Dimension of Temperament Survey. *Journal of Adolescent Research*, **1**, 213–229.

Yu, J., & Williford, W. R. (1992). The age of alcohol onset and alcohol, cigarette, and marijuana use patterns: an analysis of drug use progression of young adults in New York State. *International Journal of Addiction*, **27**, 1313–1323.

Zucker, R. A., & Harford, T. C. (1983). National study of the demography of adolescent drinking practices in 1980. *Journal of Studies on Alcohol*, **44**, 974–985.

Zucker, R. A. (2006a). The developmental behavior genetics of drug involvement: Overview and comments. *Behavior Genetics*, **36**(4), 616–625.

Zucker, R. A. (2006b). Alcohol use and alcohol use disorders: A developmental–biopsychosocial system formulation covering the life course. In D. Cicchetti & D. J. Cohen (Eds.), *Developmental psychopathology: Risk, disorder and adaptation* (Vol. 3, 2nd ed., pp. 620–656). New York: Wiley.

Zuckerman, M. (1987). Biological connection between sensation seeking and drug abuse. In J. Engel & L. Oreland (Eds.), *Brain reward systems and abuse* (pp. 165–176). New York: Raven Press.

ACKNOWLEDGMENTS

The authors acknowledge the support of grants MH42498, MH56961, MH57024, and MH57095 from the National Institute of Mental Health and DA16903 from the National Institute on Drug Abuse. Dodge is grateful for the support of Senior Scientist Award DA015226 and the Transdisciplinary Prevention Research Center P30 DA023026 from the National Institute on Drug Abuse. The authors are grateful for the contributions of numerous staff members and research participants of the Child Development Project.

TAKING SUBSTANCE USE AND DEVELOPMENT SERIOUSLY:
DEVELOPMENTALLY DISTAL AND PROXIMAL INFLUENCES ON
ADOLESCENT DRUG USE

John E. Schulenberg and Julie Maslowsky

This compelling study clearly illustrates what many of us have long
been saying, though not always as thoroughly or as convincingly, that adolescent drug use is a developmental phenomenon. Dodge et al. show how
early influences work through different systems over time, from the individual through parenting and peer relations and back to individual drug
use. That adolescent drug use is a significant national problem has not been
in question for decades; that externalizing behavior, ineffective parenting,
and association with deviant peers are risk factors for adolescent drug use is
not new; and that carefully conducted longitudinal research is essential for
advancement in the understanding of developmental processes has long
been a fact in our science. What is new and important here, for both developmental scientists and addiction researchers, is the demonstration of
how risk factors from different systems gather together sequentially across a
13-year period, how they interact systematically over time, and how each
potentiates and directs earlier risk factors to set the stage for the high likelihood of adolescent use of illicit drugs. This clear explication of cascading
effects as "the stuff of development" helps us see why we need to pay as
much attention to developmentally distal influences as we do to developmentally proximal ones. In this commentary, we offer thoughts about some
of the many strengths and contributions of the Dodge et al. study, as well as
about future considerations building on this study.

CASCADING EFFECTS

The cascading effects conceptualization that is appropriately center-
stage in this study is of critical importance. Masten et al. (2005) have been

instrumental in bringing forth this conceptualization to help us understand how development builds on itself, for better and worse, and how pathways reflect temporal and perhaps causal flow across domains. Dodge et al. take it all further by providing an integration of dynamic relations across multiple domains through childhood and adolescence. In testing their model, the authors find that each step in the developmental sequence increases the predictive value of the preceding step. In other words, adding constructs that are increasingly proximal to the outcome makes the distal measures more informative. Each step in the developmental sequence provides unique opportunities for moving toward or away from substance use, for continuing on a risky path or moving onto a less risky one. Based on this study, the work of Masten et al., and that of others, an easy prediction for us is that dynamic cascading conceptualizations and empirical efforts will continue to yield important advances about how developmentally distal and proximal influences across different domains work together to contribute to problematic and salutary outcomes.

COMPELLING FRAMEWORK AND METICULOUS MODEL TESTING

Praise and emulation are deserved for how Dodge et al. set up and conducted their model testing. The mediated models, guided by the dynamic cascade conceptualization, include hypotheses from previous research along with coercive social learning theory, transactional model, and cumulative risk model. The use of PLS appears to have some important features for a study as comprehensive as this one. Data reduction was necessary, but the wide range of relevant variables to be included was not conducive to a typical factor analysis/structural equation modeling approach. PLS allows for the creation of composite variables that maximally relate to the outcome without assuming they all indicate a single cause. This allowed the researchers to include indicators of broad categories of developmentally relevant variables such as sociodemographic risk or early parenting risk without meeting the usual requirement of high intercorrelations among the variables within a category. The use of an index rather than a factor-based construct is an important contribution of this study. Essentially, this approach is one in which the variables within the index are viewed as sufficient but not necessary for a given outcome.

Age of onset of substance use is important in terms of substance use etiology and consequences (Maggs & Schulenberg, 2005), and Dodge et al. do well by testing for variation in magnitude of the predictors as a function of age of onset. They found few significant interactions, but what they did find was quite interesting, particularly the differential effects of peer influence on substance use initiation. Several indicators of peer substance use measured in

Grades 6 and 7 showed greater prediction of initiating substance use by Grade 7 than of later initiation. This may reflect that peer influences are more contemporaneous and that they shift quickly across adolescence.

Another important aspect of the testing strategy was to examine potential gender moderation (whether the parameters were different for boys and girls). They found that parameters did not vary by gender, consistent with what others have found in terms of family, peer, and individual risk factors being invariant across gender and also race/ethnicity (e.g., Pilgrim, Schulenberg, O'Malley, Bachman, & Johnston, 2006). Particularly because many of the predictors of substance use in this model are commonly thought to predominate in boys (externalizing behavior, conduct problems), it is important to note that the results of this study indicate that such behaviors, when present in girls, represent equal risk for later substance use. Thus, although it is often the case that means vary across important subgroups, relations among variables often do not.

To pull it all together, the authors test alternative models specified a priori. The accepted final model yields an integrated and parsimonious model of the dynamic cascades across time and domains. The authors recognize that they could improve the fit of this model by adding paths, but they resist and instead remain with the a priori model. This is an infrequent but admirable approach and avoids the dangers of over-fitting models (e.g., by capitalizing on chance, the accepted model may not generalize). On the other hand, we are curious about what paths in the accepted model could be freed to improve the model fit, for they likely would yield important information about additional mediation and direct effects.

A pattern-centered approach is important for recognizing, and better yet, embracing the heterogeneity of pathways. Chapter 12 is important on a practical level because, as the authors note, clinical decisions are made on a case-by-case assessment of risk factors facing a child. Such a decision process may be justified given the consistent increase in probability of substance use with each additional risk factor. Person-centered analyses also reveal that the opposite is true; children on a high-risk track can move to a lower risk track via the absence of one or more risk factors in their developmental sequence. Such analyses illustrate, on the level of individual trajectories, that distal risks do not determine eventual outcome. Multifinality is the rule: heterogeneous pathways result from a single starting point.

Overall, this study provides an excellent "macro framework" for future studies of the development of conduct problems and substance use. Their review facilitates location of where a smaller, more in-depth study fits in the macro framework. For example, a study of a particular age group or of one or two links in the cascade model could be appropriately imbedded in the context and developmental framework provided here, enriching that study and elucidating its contribution to our understanding. Relatedly, as part of their review, the authors organized the literature to reveal those areas that have been substantially researched and those in which there is relatively little work to date. This creates a clear agenda for future research, highlighting those areas of the development of substance use in which more research is needed in order to understand fully the context of how these problems may develop. Specifically, the authors have pointed to important future directions such as the need to include more biological variables, or look for additional moderators and/or mediators in order to build upon the framework they have drawn out.

HETEROTYPIC CONTINUITY AND MEASUREMENT EQUIVALENCE

In their dynamic developmental approach, Dodge et al. make it clear that the manifestations of underlying constructs—such as ineffective parenting, externalizing behavior, peer relation difficulties—shift over time. More generally, adaptation and maladaptation tend to be continuous across time, while many of the activities and behaviors associated with adaptation tend to be discontinuous (e.g., Allen, Porter, McFarland, Marsh, & McElhaney, 2005; Cicchetti & Rogosch, 2002; Moffitt & Caspi, 2001; Rutter, 1996). This reflects heterotypic continuity (continuity in underlying purpose or function, but discontinuity in manifest behavior over time), which is distinguished from homotypic continuity (continuity in both) and functional discontinuity (manifest behavior remains continuous but purpose or function shifts over time) (Schulenberg, Maggs, & O'Malley, 2003). The particular emphasis by Dodge et al. on how ineffective parenting and peer relation difficulties shift with development of the target child is an important contribution of this study, both in terms of theoretical acknowledgment and empirical approach. And this reflects a larger and quite thorny measurement issue for developmental scientists conducting long-term longitudinal research. As a science, we are reasonably clear on the understanding of the importance of measurement equivalence, the extent to which a given construct is being measured in the same way over time (e.g., Nesselroade & Estabrook, 2009). Thus, without establishing measurement equivalence, it is difficult to know the extent to which any change we see over time relates to change in the construct versus change in the way the construct is measured. But this makes sense only when one assumes homotypic continuity, for measurement equivalence gets quite tricky for heterotypic continuity. How to handle the measurement of cross-individual and cross-time differences in manifest behavior of common constructs is receiving some attention (e.g., Nesselroade, Gerstorf, Hardy, & Ram, 2007), but much more is needed. Thus, this study helps both in giving the matter conceptual attention and working throughout empirically.

DEVELOPMENTAL TRANSITIONS

The authors give some attention to developmental transitions, beginning their study with the transition to school, and having the outcome (initiation of illicit drug use) span the transition into and across adolescence. The point is made that transitions are useful periods to include in developmental studies because they can engender instability allowing for variation of and covariation among constructs. Indeed, developmental transitions offer needed vantage points for addressing issues of continuity and discontinuity (Cicchetti & Rogosch, 2002; Rutter, 1996; Schulenberg & Zarrett, 2006). Especially when studying developmental cascades, which reflect to some extent continuity (e.g., bad circumstances set the stage for other bad circumstances), transitions are important to consider because they can interrupt ongoing person–context interactions and thus serve as turning points for better or worse. At the same time, transitions can contribute to continuity by serving as proving grounds that help consolidate and strengthen ongoing behavioral and adjustment trajectories for better and worse (Schulenberg & Zarrett, 2006). Thus, internal and social context transitions can potentiate or divert ongoing cascading influences, setting the stage for stronger or weaker developmentally distal effects. Greater attention to developmental transitions is needed in cascading studies.

THE MEASUREMENT OF ADOLESCENT DRUG USE

Dodge et al. resist a common practice of combining alcohol, tobacco, and illicit drugs into a composite measure, arguing that to do so might mask important developmental and ecological linkages to substance use onset. As Dodge et al. state, alcohol, cigarette, and illicit drug use show distinct patterns in terms of timing of onset, escalation, and decline across adolescence and into young adulthood, and these different substances show distinct historical trends in terms of peaks and declines (Johnston, O'Malley, Bachman, & Schulenberg, 2009). Focusing only on illicit drug use (including marijuana, cocaine, heroin, inhalants, and other illicit drugs) does have advantages given the purposes of this study, and combining illicit drugs into a composite measure makes good sense, though it is noteworthy that marijuana use typically accounts for most of the illicit drug use. For example, based on the 2008 national Monitoring the Future (MTF) survey of 12th graders, the prevalence rate for lifetime use of any illicit drug (including inhalants) is 49.3%, whereas the prevalence rate for lifetime use of marijuana is 42.6% (Johnston et al., 2009). But not including tobacco and alcohol use (as distinct measures) does represent a missed opportunity. Tobacco and alcohol use typically precede illicit drug use, though many who

125

use tobacco and alcohol do not continue on to illicit drug use. Understanding what, in terms of developmental cascades, contributes to crossing the line into illicit drug use is important for future research.

The decision to focus on lifetime use—that is, onset of illicit drug use—was partly a function of the inconsistent measurement of substance use across adolescence; thus lifetime use was a common denominator. Measurement issues aside, the first use of illicit drugs is obviously very meaningful. Most young people who try an illicit drug (which is typically marijuana) report using illicit drugs (again, typically marijuana) more than once or twice. For example, based on the 2008 national MTF survey of 12th graders, considering only the 42.6% who report any lifetime use of marijuana, less than one fourth of them (23.9%) use it only once or twice; thus, over three fourths move beyond the "just trying it" phase, and indeed, nearly a third (32.6%) report using it 40 or more times in their lifetime (Johnston et al., 2009). No doubt, initiation of illicit drugs is a problem and thus worthy of the in-depth attention it received by Dodge et al. Future analyses, however, would benefit by examining the deeper end of illicit drug use, including frequent use of marijuana and other harder drugs. Distinguishing between first use and more consistent and heavy use is important etiologically because each distinct pattern of use likely has different developmentally distal and proximal risk factors.

EXTENDING THE FRAMEWORK AND THE RESEARCH

The Dodge et al. study does well in embracing the complexity inherent in the understanding of human development and does equally well in taming the complexity, theoretically and empirically, so as to make it feasible. As we discussed above, their model justification, set up, and testing are admirable, and indeed the "macro framework" of the study can be useful for locating other studies. Of course, the framework can and should be extended in numerous ways. In particular, as the authors discuss, more attention should be given to biological aspects of conduct problems and substance use, specifically potential genetic contributions. Genotype is increasingly viewed as an important moderator in the effects of environment on the development of psychopathology including conduct problems and substance use (Rutter, Moffitt, & Caspi, 2006). Functional polymorphisms of the COMT, MAOA, and 5HTT genes have been implicated in the development of alcoholism (for a review, see Enoch, 2007). Genotype, particularly MAOA genotype, has also been implicated in the development of conduct problems (e.g. Caspi et al., 2002; Foley et al., 2004; Haberstick et al., 2005). The research to date has indicated that genes are especially important in predicting externalizing disorders in the context of environmental adversity (Hicks, South, Dirago, Iacono, & McGue, 2009). The Dodge et al. model identifies several sources of

environmental risk for the development of substance use and conduct problems, including poor parenting practices and sociodemographic risk. The
contributions of these environmental factors may be further clarified with the
addition of genetic information, perhaps allowing for the understanding of
how specific subgroups are more or less affected by environmental influences, depending on their genotype.

The influence of parents and peers on substance use and conduct problems is indisputable, but a third important set of contextual influences involves the school (e.g., Bachman et al., 2008). School influences dovetail with
parental influences and often serve to structure peer influences. Indeed,
without much extension of the model, one could easily imagine how difficulties and successes in school fit into the dynamic cascading process. A related
extension of the framework is to include predictors that span further into
middle and high school to capture the dynamic interactions that likely escalate
further into adolescence (which would correspond with more of a focus on
onset and escalation of more frequent illicit drug use mentioned above).

It is a truism, though one worth pushing on, that one can either conduct
a large-scale study with a large representative sample and-survey measurement or a smaller scale study with more intensive measurement necessary to
get at developmental mechanisms. To advance developmental science and
the study of addictions, doing both, or finding a way to combine both
effectively (e.g., Curran & Hussong, 2009), is needed. This is especially true
for the vein that Dodge et al. have struck. Dynamic cascades are likely to be
moderated by not just sociodemographic characteristics but also individual
characteristics; large representative samples allow for more in-depth consideration of pattern-centered analyses to discover common and unique
pathways, resilience, and multifinality (Cicchetti & Rogosch, 2002; Schulenberg & Zarrett, 2006).

CONCLUSIONS AND IMPLICATIONS

This study joins a growing list of conceptual and empirical efforts that
examine adolescent drug use as a developmental phenomenon (e.g., see
Brown et al., 2008; Chassin, Hussong, & Beltran, 2009; Maggs & Schulenberg, 2005; Masten, Faden, Zucker, & Spear, 2008; Zucker, 2006). As is
clearly recognized, understanding the etiology and course of substance use
from early on, as well as the contextual covariates and influences, is essential
for designing effective interventions. Indeed, interventions that build on a
developmental and contextual foundation, focusing on the social and individual mechanisms that set the stage for optimal development, can be
successful in reducing adolescent drug use and related problems (e.g.,
Hawkins et al., 2009; Kellam et al., 2008). Dodge et al. discuss some useful

implications for targeted intervention efforts, and more generally, one can see through this study the power of prediction that comes from thorough longitudinal screening; at the same time, given the unique contributions of more developmentally proximal cascade effects, early interventions alone are likely to be insufficient.

In sum, the authors present an elegant model of cascading influences, taking us from early parenting difficulties up through substance use initiation in adolescence. They highlight the major roles of early behavior problems and of parenting and peer problems that occur in early childhood and adolescence. They take their results further by demonstrating invariance in the relationships by gender and by demonstrating the informative heterogeneity of individual trajectories that underlie these results. The authors understand that not all the important components are included here and that other sequences and pathways are likely. Science will move forward to include other components and pathways to provide a fuller understanding of the complex net of influences on adolescent drug use that is very much needed. What will last from this study is the imagery of the underlying process—dynamic cascades—representing how developmentally distal and proximal influences across different domains work together to direct and potentiate each other toward a likely but not predetermined outcome. Theoretically and practically, this is the major contribution of the Dodge et al. study. Those of us who talk with parent and community groups and policy makers have seen a common fear that adolescent drug use "comes out of nowhere," that there are lurking contemporaneous forces over which we have little control. Developmentally informed addiction researchers and developmental scientists know this to be untrue. And to help show it is untrue, we now have the Dodge et al. study, giving us a compelling illustration of how adolescent drug use comes from known developmentally ordered forces.

ACKNOWLEDGMENT

Work on this commentary was funded in part by support from the National Institute on Drug Abuse (R01 DA 01411) and the Center for Human Growth and Development at the University of Michigan. The content here is solely the responsibility of the authors and does not necessarily represent the official views of the sponsors.

References

Allen, J. P., Porter, M. R., McFarland, F. C., Marsh, P., & McElhaney, K. B. (2005). The two faces of adolescents' success with peers: Adolescent popularity, social adaptation, and deviant behavior. *Child Development*, **76**, 747–760.

Bachman, J. G., O'Malley, P. M., Schulenberg, J. E., Johnston, L. D., Freedman-Doan, P., & Messersmith, E. E. (2008). *The education–drug use connection: How successes and failures in school relate to adolescent smoking, drinking, drug use, and delinquency.* New York: Lawrence Erlbaum Associates/Taylor & Francis.

Brown, S. A., McGue, M., Maggs, J. L., Schulenberg, J. E., Hingson, R., Swartzwelder, S., et al. (2008). A developmental perspective on alcohol and youths 16 to 20 years of age. *Pediatrics*, **121**, S290–S310.

Caspi, A., McLay, J., Moffitt, T. E., Mill, J., Martin, J., Craig, I. W., et al. (2002). Role of genotype in the cycle of violence in maltreated children. *Science*, **297**, 851–854.

Chassin, L., Hussong, A., & Beltran, I. (2009). Adolescent substance use. In R. M. Lerner & L. Steinberg (Eds.), *Handbook of adolescent psychology* (3rd ed., pp. 723–763). New York: Wiley.

Cicchetti, D., & Rogosch, F. A. (2002). A developmental psychopathology perspective on adolescence. *Journal of Consulting and Clinical Psychology*, **70**(1), 6–20.

Curran, P. J., & Hussong, A. M. (2009). Integrative data analysis: The simultaneous analysis of multiple data sets. *Psychological Methods*, **14**, 81–100.

Enoch, M. A. (2007). Genetic and environmental influences on the development of alcoholism: Resilience versus risk. *Annals of the New York Academy of Science*, **1094**, 193–201.

Foley, D. L., Eaves, L. J., Wormley, B., Silberg, J. L., Maes, H. H., Kuhn, J., et al. (2004). Childhood adversity, monoamine oxidase A genotype, and risk for conduct disorder. *Archives of General Psychiatry*, **61**, 738–744.

Haberstick, B., Lessem, J., Hopfer, C., Smolen, A., Ehringer, M., Timberlake, D., et al. (2005). Monoamine oxidase A (MAOA) and antisocial behaviors in the presence of childhood and adolescent maltreatment. *American Journal of Medical Genetics: Neuropsychiatric Genetics*, **135**, 59–64.

Hawkins, J. D., Oesterle, S., Brown, E. C., Arthur, M. W., Abbott, R. D., Fagain, A. A., et al. (2009). Results of a type 2 translational research trial to prevent adolescent drug use and delinquency. *Archives of Pediatric and Adolescent Medicine*, **163**, 789–798.

Hicks, B. M., South, S. C., Dirago, A. C., Iacono, W. G., & McGue, M. (2009). Environmental adversity and increasing genetic risk for externalizing disorders. *Archives of General Psychiatry*, **66**, 640–648.

Johnston, L. D., O'Malley, P. M., Bachman, J. G., & Schulenberg, J. E. (2009). *Monitoring the Future national survey results on drug use, 1975–2008. Volume I: Secondary school students* (NIH Publication No. 09-7402). Bethesda, MD: National Institute on Drug Abuse.

Kellam, S. G., Brown, C. H., Poduska, J. M., Ialongo, N. S., Wang, W., Toyinbo, P., et al. (2008). Effects of a universal classroom behavior management program in first and second grades on young adult behavioral, psychiatric, and social outcomes. *Drug and Alcohol Dependence*, **95S**, S5–S28.

Maggs, J. L., & Schulenberg, J. E. (2005). Initiation and course of alcohol consumption among adolescents and young adults. In M. Galanter (Ed.), *Recent developments in alcoholism. Vol. 17: Alcohol problems in adolescents and young adults* (pp. 29–47). New York: Kluwer Academic/Plenum Publishers.

Masten, A. S., Faden, V. B., Zucker, R. A., & Spear, L. P. (2008). Underage drinking: A developmental framework. *Pediatrics*, **121**, S235–S251.

Masten, A. S., Roisman, G. I., Long, J. D., Burt, K. B., Obradović, J., Riley, J. R., et al. (2005). Developmental cascades: Linking academic achievement, externalizing and internalizing symptoms over 20 years. *Developmental Psychology*, **41**, 733–746.

Moffitt, T. E., & Caspi, A. (2001). Childhood predictors differentiate life-course persistent and adolescence-limited antisocial pathways among males and females. *Development and Psychopathology*, **13**, 355–375.

Nesselroade, J. R., & Estabrook, R. (2009). Factor invariance, measurement, and studying development over the lifespan. In H. Bosworth & C. Hertzog (Ed.), *Aging and cognition: Research methodologies and empirical advances* (pp. 39–52). Washington, DC: American Psychological Association.

Nesselroade, J. R., Gerstorf, D., Hardy, S. A., & Ram, N. (2007). Idiographic filters for psychological constructs. *Measurement: Interdisciplinary Research and Perspectives*, **5**, 217–235.

Pilgrim, C. C., Schulenberg, J. E., O'Malley, P. M., Bachman, J. G., & Johnston, L. D. (2006). Mediators and moderators of parental involvement on substance use: A national study of adolescents. *Prevention Science*, **10**, 1–15.

Rutter, M. (1996). Transitions and turning points in developmental psychopathology: As applied to the age span between childhood and mid-adulthood. *International Journal of Behavioral Development*, **19**(3), 603–626.

Rutter, M., Moffitt, T., & Caspi, A. (2006). Gene-environment interplay and psychopathology: multiple varieties but real effects. *Journal of Child Psychology and Psychiatry*, **47**, 226–261.

Schulenberg, J., Maggs, J. L., & O'Malley, P. M. (2003). How and why the understanding of developmental continuity and discontinuity is important: The sample case of long-term consequences of adolescent substance use. In J. T. Mortimer & M. J. Shanahan (Eds.), *Handbook of the life course* (pp. 413–436). New York: Kluwer Academic/Plenum Publishers.

Schulenberg, J. E., & Zarrett, N. R. (2006). Mental health during emerging adulthood: Continuity and discontinuity in courses, causes, and functions. In J. J. Arnett & J. L. Tanner (Eds.), *Emerging adults in America: Coming of age in the 21st century* (pp. 135–172). Washington, DC: American Psychological Association.

Zucker, R. A. (2006). Alcohol use and alcohol use disorders: A developmental-biopsycho-social system formulation covering the life course. In D. Cicchetti & D. J. Cohen (Eds.), *Developmental psychopathology: Risk, disorder and adaptation* (2nd ed., pp. 620–656). New York: Wiley.

CONTRIBUTORS

Kenneth A. Dodge is the William McDougall Professor of Public Policy and Professor of Psychology and Neuroscience at Duke University, where he directs the Center for Child and Family Policy. His research is aimed at understanding how problem behaviors develop and how they can be prevented.

Patrick S. Malone is Associate Professor of Psychology at The University of South Carolina. As a quantitative social psychologist, he utilizes advanced methodological techniques to address substantive questions of social risk for substance use outcomes.

Jennifer E. Lansford is Associate Research Professor at the Duke University Center for Child and Family Policy. Her research focuses on how family, peer, and cultural contexts affect the development of aggression and other behavior problems in youth.

Shari Miller is Research Scientist at the Research Triangle Institute. She is supported by an NIMH K Award to study antisocial development in girls.

Gregory S. Pettit is Human Sciences Professor of Child Development at Auburn University. His research focuses on the mechanisms through which family and peer experiences exert an impact on child-developmental outcomes and on the risk and protective factors that moderate these linkages.

John E. Bates is Professor of Psychological and Brain Sciences at Indiana University. One major focus of his research is on how children's characteristics interact with characteristics of their environments in shaping the development of psychopathology versus positive adjustments.

John E. Schulenberg is Professor of Psychology and Research Professor at the Institute for Social Research and Center for Human Growth and

Development. His research focuses on psychosocial development during adolescence and young adulthood, with specific emphasis on the link between developmental transitions and health and well-being, on alcohol and other drug use, on developmental intervention and prevention research, and on the conceptualization and analysis of change. Using nationally representative, multiwave, longitudinal samples, his topics of interest are the increase in health risks during adolescence, the description and explanation of trajectories of substance use during adolescence and young adulthood, discontinuities in functioning and adjustment during the transition to young adulthood, the comorbidity of substance use and psychopathology during adolescence and adulthood, and the combination of variable-centered and pattern-centered approaches to maximize understanding of developmental change.

Julie Maslowsky is a Developmental Graduate Student. Maslowky is interested in using both biological and psychosocial measures to delineate mechanisms of formation of psychopathology versus well-being in childhood and adolescence and, in doing so, to gain knowledge for use in informing and formulating prevention and intervention programs for high-risk populations.

STATEMENT OF EDITORIAL POLICY

The *Monographs* series aims to publish major reports of developmental research that generate authoritative new findings and uses these to foster a fresh perspective or integration of findings on some conceptually significant issue. Submissions from programmatic research projects are welcomed; these may consist of individually or group-authored reports of findings from a single large-scale investigation or from a sequence of experiments centering on a particular question. Multiauthored sets of independent studies that center on the same underlying question may also be appropriate; a critical requirement in such instances is that the various authors address common issues and that the contribution arising from the set as a whole be unique, substantial, and well-integrated. Manuscripts reporting interdisciplinary or multidisciplinary research on significant developmental questions and those including evidence from diverse cultural, racial, ethnic, national, or other contexts are of particular interest. Because the aim of the series is not only to advance knowledge on specialized topics but also to enhance cross-fertilization among disciplines or subfields, the links between the specific issues under study and larger questions relating to developmental processes should emerge clearly for both general readers and specialists on the topic. In short, irrespective of how it may be framed, work that contributes significant data or extends developmental thinking will be considered.

Potential authors are not required to be members of the Society for Research in Child Development or affiliated with the academic discipline of psychology to submit a manuscript for consideration by the *Monographs*. The significance of the work in extending developmental theory and in contributing new empirical information is the crucial consideration.

Submissions should contain a minimum of 80 manuscript pages (including tables and references). The upper boundary of 150–175 pages is more flexible, but authors should try to keep within this limit. If color artwork is submitted, and the authors believe color art is necessary to the presentation of their work, the submissions letter should indicate that one or more authors or their institutions are prepared to pay the substantial costs associated with color art reproduction. Please submit manuscripts electronically to the SRCD Monographs Online Submissions and Review Site (MONOSubmit) at www.srcd.org/monosubmit. Please contact the Monographs office with any questions at monographs@srcd.org.

The corresponding author for any manuscript must, in the submission letter, warrant that all coauthors are in agreement with the content of the manuscript. The corresponding author also is responsible for informing all coauthors, in a timely manner, of manuscript submission, editorial decisions, reviews received, and any revisions recommended. Before publication, the corresponding author must warrant in the submissions letter that the study was conducted according to the ethical guidelines of the Society for Research in Child Development.

Potential authors who may be unsure whether the manuscript they are planning would make an appropriate submission are invited to draft an outline of what they propose and send it to the editor for assessment. This mechanism, as well as a more detailed description of all editorial policies, evaluation processes, and format requirements, is given in the "Guidelines for the Preparation of Publication Submissions," which can be found at the SRCD website by clicking on *Monographs*, or by contacting the editor, W. Andrew Collins, Institute of Child Development, University of Minnesota, 51 E. River Road, Minneapolis, MN 55455-0345; e-mail: wcollins@umn.edu.

Note to NIH Grantees

Pursuant to NIH mandate, Society through Wiley-Blackwell will post the accepted version of Contributions authored by NIH grantholders to PubMed Central upon acceptance. This accepted version will be made publicly available 12 months after publication. For further information, see www.wiley.com/go/nihmandate.

CURRENT